Social Policies
for the Elderly in the
Third World

Recent Titles in
Contributions to the Study of Aging

SOCIAL POLICIES FOR THE ELDERLY IN THE THIRD WORLD

Martin B. Tracy

Contributions to the Study of Aging, Number 22
Erdman B. Palmore, *Series Adviser*

GREENWOOD PRESS
New York • Westport, Connecticut • London

Library of Congress Cataloging-in-Publication Data

Tracy, Martin.
  Social policies for the elderly in the third world / Martin B.
Tracy.
      p.   cm.—(Contributions to the study of aging, ISSN
  0732–085X ; no. 22)
  Includes bibliographical references and index.
  ISBN 0–313–26377–9 (alk. paper)
  1. Old age assistance—Developing countries. 2. Aged—Government
policy—Developing countries.   I. Title.   II. Series.
HV1494.T73   1991
362.6′09172′4—dc20   90–45605

British Library Cataloguing in Publication Data is available.

Library of Congress Catalog Card Number: 90–45605
ISBN: 0–313–26377–9
ISSN: 0732–085X

First published in 1991

Greenwood Press, 88 Post Road West, Westport, CT   06881
An imprint of Greenwood Publishing Group, Inc.

Printed in the United States of America

∞

The paper used in this book complies with the
Permanent Paper Standard issued by the National
Information Standards Organization (Z39.48–1984).

10 9 8 7 6 5 4 3 2 1

To Patsy and Morgan,
who make my life joyful and adventuresome.

Contents

Acknowledgments

Throughout a career as a government employee with the U.S. Social Security Administration, as a research analyst with the International Social Security Association, and as a teacher at the University of Iowa, I have had great fortune in working with and for individuals who have been more than generous in giving of their time and effort to attempt to instruct me in the basic skills of understanding social welfare policies in a cross-national context. Theirs has not been an easy task and they have been most tolerant of my frequent requests for guidance and assistance. I can only hope that this book speaks well of their good counsel. Readers are advised that whatever errors of judgment or content that may occur in the text do not necessarily reflect the opinions or instructions of my mentors or collaborators.

I wish to acknowledge a number of friends and colleagues, from whom I have learned much and to whom I owe more, who have been instrumental in laying the foundation for this study. These include Max Horlick, former Chief of the Comparative Studies Staff of the U.S. Social Security Administration and currently an editor of *International Benefits Information Service* (IBIS); the late Christine Cockburn, past Director of the Research Section of the International Social Security Association; Vladimir Rys, Secretary-General of the International Social Security Association; Professor Richard Merritt, Political Science Department of the University of Illinois at Champaign-Urbana; and Merlin Taber, School of Social Work at the University of Illinois.

I am grateful to those who have generously shared their knowledge in reading drafts of the country chapters (noted in parentheses) included in the text: Professor Z. Chuanyi, Institute of American Studies, Chinese Academy of Social Sciences, Beijing (Peoples' Republic of China), Professor P. K. B. Nayar, former Chair of the Department of Sociology at the University of Kerala (Kerala, India); Professor Margaret Peil, Centre of West African Studies, Birmingham University, England (Nigeria); and M. Nuri Arslan, General Manager of the Turkish Employment Organization (Turkey); and Lisa Walz, M. S. W. and Professor Tom Walz, Iowa City, Iowa for their valuable assistance with material on Mexico. I am especially grateful to Dr. Nayar, whose sponsorship as a Visiting Fellow at the University of Kerala provided me with a wonderful opportunity to test my research model on a firsthand basis.

Professor Paul Greenough, Director of the Center for International and Comparative Studies (CICS) of the University of Iowa was instrumental in helping me to develop important professional contacts in India. CICS provided financial support for information-gathering trips to Trivandrum, India, and Geneva, Switzerland. I also appreciate the input of colleagues at the seminar on International Health and Social Services at the University of Iowa.

I am indebted to colleagues who read various drafts of the manuscript and were thoughtful enough to be critical in their observations and considerate enough not to be discouraging: Professor James Midgley, Dean, School of Social Work, Louisiana State University; Charlotte Nusberg, Secretary-General, International Federation on Ageing, Washington, D.C.; and Professor Patsy D. Tracy, Division of Social Sciences, Mount Mercy College, Cedar Rapids, Iowa. I am also grateful to Barbara Yerkes for her assistance in editing the text.

Introduction

This book introduces a problem-solving model to cross-national studies of social programs for the elderly in economically developing nations—the Third World, a term that is used here only as a designation of unspecified relatively lower levels of industrial and economic development. Current models of cross-national analysis tend to focus on theory testing and description; they fail to provide the practical information that indigenous policymakers need to decide whether another nation's policy, program, or provision is appropriate to their own country.

CURRENT MODELS

Academic cross-national studies of social welfare programs typically use two general frameworks of analysis, both best suited to studies of economically developed societies. In one approach, descriptive research compares the development of social programs across nations, examining expenditures and technical provisions. In the few cases where Third World nations are included in such studies, the level of development is usually a measure of the extent to which industrial models have been adopted.

Thus, comparisons are usually based on the degree of social insurance coverage for lost-income contingencies associated with industrialization and a wage economy—that is, work injury, unemployment, sickness, disability, retirement, and death. These descriptive studies examine such variables as the type of workers covered, benefit levels, replacement rates, retirement age, age of first awards, and qualifying conditions.[1]

In the second comparative approach, researchers test "grand" or macro social, political, and economic theories of development (industrial, political, and class theories; theories of convergence and diffusion). Using aggregate data bases, these studies correlate specific political and economic indicators, including social program expenditures, political parties and interest groups, government legislatures, economic data, demographic data, age of programs, and the level of benefits. With few exceptions, the theory-building literature has studied events and patterns in industrial societies.[2]

Apart from these academic studies, another body of cross-national research is produced by professional staff members of international agencies and advisory bodies that provide technical information and assistance. Among the more widely known of these agencies are the International Labour Office (ILO), the International Social Security Association (ISSA), the World Health Organization (WHO), the Office of International Policy (OIP) of the U.S. Social Security Administration (SSA), the Pan American Health Organization (PAHO), the International Federation on Ageing (IFA), the American Association for International Aging (AAIA), and the Center for International Research (CIR) of the U.S. Census Bureau.

Like academic researches, these organizations perform descriptive studies of programs, but they usually compare the program features and expenditure levels of social programs in nations at similar stages of economic development. At the more analytical level, these organizations study the specialized and technical aspects of programs, with the goal of making them more efficient and effective.

While all of these research approaches help advance social welfare programs, they do not provide a method that serves the pragmatic interests of national planners and policymakers of Third World nations. A policymaker who turns to a textbook for a clearly structured method of analyzing how developing countries approach social welfare policy issues and problems is going to be disappointed.

PROCESS MODEL

To meet the needs of policymakers and international consultants, this text focuses on the comparative information that should be most useful to a government choosing among pragmatic approaches to an identified need. Thus, a government setting social welfare policies for the elderly should understand how such programs have developed in other countries. It can then judge whether all or part of another nation's program would be transferable to its own circumstances.

Policymakers need answers to questions such as these: What social, economic, and political circumstances led to specific government programs and provisions? What goals and objectives are the programs and provisions designed to accomplish? What is the strategic value of a program or provision in addressing the social issues associated with aging populations, including poverty, access to services, family responsibilities, institutionalization, and provision for health care?

To provide answers without becoming bogged down in costly and time-consuming theoretical studies, the model provided here generates the facts that are most relevant to problem-solving. It asks nine questions about the program of the government of the country under study. The questions inquire about the government's formal responsibility for and philosophical perspective on social welfare:

- What is the government's legal or constitutional authority in providing social welfare, including programs for the elderly?

- What is the dominant conceptual (ideological) position regarding government intervention in providing social welfare?

Answers to these two inquiries enable the analyst to assess the government's bona fide commitment to a program or provision, an important indication of whether the program will transfer to a nation where (because of legal or ideological conditions) it is likely to be greater or less.

The remaining questions focus on the process of adopting a specific policy, program, or provision that affects benefits and services for the elderly:

- What factors were the greatest obstacles to government involvement in the particular policy, program, or provision under review?

- What factors acted as catalysts to promote government intervention?

- How did the government define the problem, identify issues, and assess needs?

- What were the government's goals and strategies?

- What form did the intervention take and how was the program implemented and administered?

- How effectively has the program addressed the identified problem and met the specified objectives?

- What are the implications of analysis for policy?

These questions do not presume that a nation necessarily follows a systematic problem-solving process. They merely suggest that a diagnosis of the context in which a strategy has been formulated is critical to making an informed decision about its applicability to another context.

TEXT OUTLINE

The text encompasses four major areas. The first discusses the challenge facing Third World societies as their elderly populations increase and as traditional sources of support for the elderly are threatened. Of particular interest are the social factors that shape governments' perceptions of the issue, prevailing attitudes toward solutions formulated in industrial countries, and internal and external pressure for governments to take action.

The second area, Chapter 2, describes in detail the analytical model. This chapter also reviews the current literature and the research methods used in comparing Third World social programs.

The third area, Chapters 3 through 7, illustrates and applies the model through case studies of four countries—the People's Republic of China, Mexico, Nigeria, and Turkey, as well as the state of Kerala in India. At the end of each chapter, the public old-age pension system for the country in question is summarized.

In each of these societies, programs for the elderly have some dominant characteristic that makes them of interest. China decentralizes the responsibility for benefits and services. In Kerala the government provides social assistance programs for the elderly. In Mexico, the government has a social and constitutional obligation to provide benefits to all the elderly, an obligation that is difficult to fulfill in the face of Mexico's enormous fiscal and administrative problems. In Nigeria, the government takes a laissez-faire approach in an attempt to maintain traditional family responsibility for the care of the elderly. The Turkish government is increasing its involvement in programs for the elderly in planned phases.

The final area, Chapter 8, summarizes and synthesizes the major findings of the case studies, isolating trends and patterns.

NOTES

1. Numerous examples of descriptive cross-national research on programs for the elderly are available in the *International Social Security Review*, published by the International Social Security Association, and in

periodic issues of the *Social Security Bulletin*, published by the U.S. Social Security Administration.

2. Readers interested in learning more about the theoretical basis of cross-national studies are referred to two edited texts: *Comparative Policy Research: Learning from Experience* (Dierkes, Weiler & Antal, 1987) and *Comparative Social Policy: Theories, Methods, Findings* (Wilensky et al., 1985). The following analyses are also recommended: Hardiman & Midgley (1989), Heidenheimer (1986), Mesa-Lago (1986), Midgley (1984b), Myles (1984), Pampel & Williamson (1985), and Williamson & Pampel (1986). Readers may also wish to refer to the list of suggested readings at the end of the text.

1

The Challenge of Government Intervention

Most Third World governments now recognize that their elderly populations will increasingly require skillful policy decisions and program strategies. The talents of policymakers will be stretched to generate programs that satisfactorily address pressing needs without weakening traditional social institutions and customs. They will be challenged by severely limited financial resources that are targeted for other population groups who are perceived as more needy or more deserving of government support.

Elderly persons represent less than 10% of the population in most Third World countries, a smaller proportion than in industrial nations, where in 1985 the elderly ranged from 10% (Japan) to 16.9% (Sweden) of the population (Torrey, Kinsella, & Taeuber, 1987). Of the world population of 1.2 billion elderly persons projected for 2025, however, 71% will live in developing regions. Moreover, the age dependency ratio (the ratio of the population over age 64 to the population 15 to 64) will rise in developing regions from 7% in 1950 to 12% in 2025 (Economic and Social Council, 1989).

In addition, the number of persons, mostly women, age 80 and over is growing very rapidly. By 2025 there will be 79 million very old women in developing countries, a growth factor of fifteen; the growth factor for the elderly population as a whole is eight (Economic and Social Council, 1989). These women are very likely to be impoverished; together with woman-headed households, they constitute 70% of the poor in most countries of the world (Seager & Olson, 1986).

These data are sufficient reason for governments to worry about how their societies will cope and what role government will play. The decisions these societies make is of importance to those who are engaged worldwide in the planning or delivery of social, health, and income services to the elderly.

It is becoming evident, moreover, that aging policy issues in the Third World are different from and more difficult to solve than the same issues in more economically developed nations, if only because the solutions that grew out of the economies and cultures of the industrial world are not always viable in the agricultural economies of the Third World.

DISADVANTAGES TO INDUSTRIAL COUNTRY MODELS

Where industrial models of government programs for the elderly have been adopted in developing nations, they are typically confined to retirement pensions for male workers employed by large industries in urban areas. Although there are scant reliable data for most Third World nations, indications are that those covered for old-age income are seldom more than a marginal percentage of the elderly. The best estimates suggest that there is an even smaller percentage of older persons protected by special health and social service programs like those that prevail in First World economies.

Absence of Prerequisites for Industrial Models

Most Third World countries lack the social and economic prerequisites that would make it possible to adopt industrial models of income, health, and social service programs. Their labor markets and social service administrative infrastructures cannot support social policies comparable to those in industrial nations.

Few Third World governments have the capacity to collect revenues and dispense benefits in the manner of industrial governments, because it requires a system that can effectively obtain taxes from employees and employers. Further, economically developing nations do not have a sufficient proportion of their population engaged in full-time wage-related employment to support programs that are based on principles of social insurance—that is, payroll contributions, as in most industrial nations.

In rural societies with primarily agricultural economies, the majority of workers are self-employed and migrant; their jobs are seasonal and not wage-based. Urban growth brings them no closer to the elementary criteria for social insurance: many urban workers have little or no employment, low wage levels, and, increasingly, unreported income. Moreover, despite an increase in the number of urban dwellers, the Third World nations of Asia, Oceania, and Africa remain predominantly agricultural and rural.

Thus, the proportion of the population engaged in full-time wage-related employment is not large enough to support social programs through payroll contribution—the administrative basis of social insurance in industrialized nations. Under any of these conditions, it is almost impossible to collect contributions to support a social insurance fund to finance health, social services, and income programs for the elderly.

In addition, the ability to implement social programs in either urban or rural areas is often deterred by a widespread mistrust of government. In many Third World societies, political influence is exercised principally in local-level patron-client networks. This tradition inhibits governments from developing nationwide, equally distributed social welfare systems (Clark, 1982).

Declining Confidence in the Fiscality of Social Insurance

An additional impetus for prudence is the crisis in social insurance funding in economically developed countries, a problem that has been the subject of numerous international studies and conferences over the past 20 years. If wealthy industrial nations have continuing problems in financing their social security systems, developing nations, which have infinitely fewer resources, are less likely to be able to implement systems on the same model.

Cultural Divergence

The results of formal and informal inquiries by Third World analysts into social and cultural developments relative to aging populations in industrial societies have also been less than reassuring. Some analysts have expressed considerable concern about the potential deleterious effects of industrial welfare models on national attitudes regarding older persons. These analysts raise serious questions as to whether the policies of industrial nations relative to aging populations result in conditions that are acceptable to the cultures of economically developing nations.

Shifting Interests

All these issues discourage economically developing societies from adopting or expanding a program modeled on those of industrialized nations. Still, Third World analysts remain interested in the concepts and mechanisms of the social insurance programs of industrial societies, in the expectation that they might adopt some aspects of these systems without negative effect. For example, they are interested in the old-age pension systems of industrial nations, particularly the experiments in Europe and the United States combining government, individual, and private industry-supported programs. These systems are striving to ensure that the basic needs of the elderly are met while maintaining the fiscal solvency of public programs

Of most interest to many Third World observers is how program diversity in industrial societies affects community and family responsibility for care of the elderly. Third World countries have a tradition of family and community support for their elderly, a tradition they fear to lose if they expand industrial social welfare models. A convincing case can be made that many industrial societies have similar fears, but Third World nations give them a higher priority. To many Third World observers it seems that current discussions among industrial governments to redistribute responsibility to care for the elderly to community and families while minimizing government intervention is something that Third World societies already have, but may be in jeopardy of losing if industrial models of policy are implemented.

The dilemma, from the Third World perspective, is how to offer support through federal and state programs without destroying the traditional responsibility of families to care for their elderly members. The critical question for policymakers is what kinds of affordable government programs can meet the basic needs of the elderly and, at the same time, encourage individual, family, community, and private-sector initiatives?

ISSUE BACKGROUND

The World Assembly on Aging, held in Vienna in 1982, provided the first clear evidence that national governments and international bodies had identified aging populations as a major worldwide social concern. The issue of aging had been raised as early as 1948 in the United Nations General Assembly at the initiation of Argentina. In 1950 the sixth session of the Social Commission considered a Report of the Secretary-General on "Welfare of the Aged: Old Age Rights." The topic was again raised by the General Assembly 1969 and was discussed throughout the 1970s. The General Assembly arranged in 1978 to organize the World Assembly for 1982 "as a forum to launch an international action programme aimed at guaranteeing economic and social security to older persons, as well as opportunities to contribute to national development" (UNOV/CSDHA, undated:2).

The World Assembly on Aging was attended by over 1,100 delegates from 124 member states, international bodies, and nongovernment organizations. Mounting interest in aging issues was evident from the activities of various regional meetings that preceded the World Assembly and from the participation of 52 developing countries. The Assembly produced the *Vienna International Plan of Action on Aging* (United Nations, 1983), which made 62 recommendations for formulating international, national, and regional policies and programs. The plan designated the United Nations Office at the Vienna/Centre for Social Development and Humanitarian Affairs (UNOV/CSDHA) as the focal point on aging in the UN system (United Nations, 1983; Anstee, 1989).

As the Plan of Action recognized, the gradual trend toward aging in some developing countries is not a prominent issue in nations where overall economic and social development needs were pressing. However, projections clearly showed that these nations would be affected by a marked increase in the population over age 60, and especially the population age 80 and over, in the near future. It was further noted that women would increasingly constitute the majority of these elderly populations (United Nations, 1983).

The World Assembly on Aging also increased awareness that large-scale migration of the middle generations into urban centers could transform villages into communities of young and old (American Association for International Aging, 1985). Migration to urban areas has increased the hardships faced by young, single mothers and low-income people who have lost the protection of extended family and community ties (Swantz, 1985, cited in Omari, 1987).

It has been suggested that four perceptions of the elderly may influence programs in developing nations (Treas & Logue, 1986). First, where resources are scarce the needs of the elderly may be seen as low in priority. Second, the aged may be seen as impediments to development because they drain valuable resources and are resistant to changes required for economic growth. Third, the aged may become victims of modernization, since their status may decline unless action is taken to preserve traditional respect. Fourth, and more positively, the aged may be seen as a resource: they are likely to work in marginal industries and public welfare services, to perform housework and child care services, and to communicate traditional skills to younger persons.

FAMILY SUPPORT

Of all the policy issues that have been the focus of attention since the World Assembly, the most important for economically developing nations is the effect of changing demographics on family support systems. Demographic changes pose challenges to which families and society have inadequate resources to respond. Moreover, government policies and programs might accelerate the decline of family support, the traditional means of meeting the needs of the elderly.

These concerns are seriously aggravated by two competing myths about the treatment of the elderly in developing and developed societies. According to one myth, older persons in developing nations are always well cared for by their families. According to the other, the elderly in industrial nations have been abandoned by their families to government institutions (Omari, 1987; Martin, 1988; Gibson & Coppard, 1989). Both myths tend to deny the need for government intervention in supplying income, health care, and social service needs of the elderly.

In reality, of course, many families in both industrial and developing countries do not have the resources to meet the needs of elderly members (Chawla, 1988; Economic and Social Council, 1989), especially low-income families and those with functionally impaired elderly. Moreover, because we have little empirical knowledge of what family dynamics and filial piety were in the past, we cannot accurately compare the extent of family support yesterday and today (Martin, 1989). Indeed, we have little data on what the current situation is in developing countries. As a result, the myths continue to be debated and remain factors in decisionmaking.

Various studies have shown that families in industrial nations maintain their intimacy and continue to assist older family members (Kendig, 1987). Yet many policymakers in developing nations believe that this is not true; they fear that if they base their programs on those of industrialized nations, their own elderly are likely to be institutionalized. This fear continues to be a prime influence in many developing nations (Chawla, 1988).

It is also documented that with the introduction of a money-based economy and new forms of social and political control, elders have lost authority, political power, and economic security (Pathmarajah, 1984; Rwezaura, 1989). As one observer has expressed it, "old age [has become] a disability as well as an economic risk" (Rwezaura, 1989:6). While the elderly of postindustrial societies have become a major political force with greater economic security than ever before, this has not yet been the experience of economically developing nations.

Because these issues are prominent, international organizations have emphasized that government programs must be specifically designed to strengthen families ("National Perspectives on Aging Issues", 1982; United Nations, 1983; American Association for International Aging, 1985; Economic and Social Council, 1989). Although the public resources to assist families in caring for their elderly are scarce, governments are beginning to view public assistance as cost-effective. If the family is unable to care for the elderly, there will presumably be greater demands for more costly publicly supported care (Gibson & Coppard, 1989; Heisel, 1989a).

2

A Framework for Cross-National Policy Process Analysis

Most governments have access to information on how other nations have dealt with the social and economic problems of aging populations. They use this information, obtained from national and international agencies, for several purposes: to evaluate their own needs for social programs; to compare their program goals, objectives, technical features, and administrative functions to those in place elsewhere; and to strengthen their efforts to redistribute income and meet social welfare and health care delivery goals.

It is not unusual for the government of one nation to adopt a feature of another's program, generally modifying that feature to meet the special program needs of the adoptive country. Industrial nations are much more likely to exchange information and adopt program features than are the nations of the Third World, but such activity is growing among Third World governments (MacPherson & Midgley, 1987).

International bodies also use this comparative information in establishing global conventions. Member nations of the International Labour Organization, for instance, use the information in setting minimum program standards for labor activities and old-age pensions. The World Health Organization uses it in determining international standards for health care delivery. This information is also essential for international bilateral and regional agreements on old-age pensions for special groups such as migrant workers.

PREVIOUS CROSS-NATIONAL RESEARCH

Focus on Industrial Nations

For a variety of practical reasons and professional biases, most cross-national research on social policy for the aging examines programs in industrial nations. In Western Europe, Canada, and the United States, programs providing income, health care, and social services have a relatively long history and are well developed, making them attractive subjects of research for social planners and academics alike. Documents and data are generally available, and the languages and cultures are familiar to the analysts. There is also a bias that the experiences of industrial nations have more to teach us about program competence, applicability, and transferability than do those of less-developed nations.

In spite of this research tendency, data that are conducive to cross-national analysis are often difficult to obtain even from economically developed countries. Data categories have no standardized definitions, and data are not uniformly maintained and recorded. Among the most extensive efforts to correct these problems are the ILO's (1988) collection of the "Cost of Social Security" and the Luxembourg Income Study's undertaking to collect, collate, and computerize comprehensive social and economic indicators (Smeeding & Torrey, 1987). Nevertheless, there is still no universally accepted methodology for maintaining and collecting data, nor do researchers agree on the most important variables or the best models for analyzing cross-national social policy data.

Data Collection in the Third World

Outside of certain United Nations agencies, researchers have devoted little attention to issues of the elderly in Third World nations. The small percentage of elderly in the populations of most Third World societies indicates, at first glance, that they represent relatively unimportant policy issues. These elderly populations have not yet reached the point where government intervention seems as necessary as it does in policies for youth, economic development, and primary health care.

There is also a perception that social programs for the elderly exist largely in urban areas and serve proportionately few workers. This perception deters research because the programs are viewed as having only a marginal impact on government policies affecting economic or social development in the country.

It is difficult, too, to obtain accurate and reliable demographic, policy, and program data. These data are not always published; they may be available only to a few authorized public officials; they may not be aggregated; they are often contradictory, with portions of the data maintained by different offices that are distant from each other; the data of one office or agency may not be compatible with that of another; and, in some cases, data are simply not collected by the agency responsible for program administration.

Moreover, researchers have trouble securing financial support from institutes for travel and extended stays in nations where there is no legacy of research. Governments in economically developing countries may withhold permission to conduct empirical studies. Analysts from industrial nations also seem to avoid conducting research on the elderly in societies in which cultural disparities or noncomparable stages of economic and social development make it difficult to apply the industrial experience.

A more subtle, but equally important, impediment to Third World research is the notion that the demographic and social issues relative to their elderly are merely symptoms of industrial societies at early stages of economic development. That is, observers assume that the issues can be understood in light of the earlier experiences of industrial nations. The literature often reflects the belief that Third World governments must merely decide how to implement social security and social service programs that have proven to be effective in Europe and North America. If this were the case, there would be little justification for investigating the idiosyncratic social and economic forces that shape policies for the elderly in the Third World.

These disincentives to research are easy to list but hard to accept without question. We have no unequivocal documentation, for example, that old-age insurance coverage is too limited to be of significance for policy analysis. Although international analysts generally accept the statement that public old-age pensions in the Third World cover a negligible proportion of workers, there is little empirical data to indicate the actual extent of coverage. The data may exist, but there have been few systematic and successful attempts to collect them. There simply are no data sources that provide comprehensive information on cash and social service benefits for the elderly in most Third World nations.

Status of Third World Research

Extant research lacks not only aggregated data but also a structured approach to cross-national policy analysis. Without such structure, Third World policymakers and international advisors have difficulty in determining the advisability of adopting, in whole or in part, another nation's policy, program, or provision. I will review first the academic and then the professional literature that does exist, noting its basic strengths and weaknesses in addressing the needs of policy planners.

Academic Research. Academic studies on the elderly in the Third World principally test theories that predict trends and patterns in the development of programs. By far the majority focus on social insurance schemes, especially the economic aspects of old-age pensions. Many of these attempt to demonstrate how pension policies are influenced by macro socioeconomic hypotheses, including theories of convergence, diffusion, and industrialization as well as incremental and structuralist theories (see Collier & Messick, 1975; Hardiman & Midgley, 1982, 1989; MacPherson & Midgley, 1987; Midgley, 1984a, 1984b; Neysmith & Edwardh, 1984; Williamson & Pampel, 1986; Wilensky, et al, 1985).

A few comparative studies of pension policies in the Third World focus on political variables, analyzing program development as a reaction to internal and external partisan pressures. For example, in studying Latin American social security programs, Mesa-Lago (1978) has investigated how trade unions and political groups have influenced pension policy. The role of international advisory agencies has also been studied.

Studies of income maintenance programs for the elderly in the Third World have described and analyzed variables that are useful for comparing the level of development of one country's pension scheme to another's. These variables include coverage, qualifying conditions, benefit formulas, average benefit amounts, pensionable age, funding, government expenditures, replacement rates, and the like. Data on these fundamental features of various systems allow analysts to determine the current status of programs across nations and to see how various national schemes have evolved. They also provide a very valuable knowledge base for policymakers, planners, and international advisors.

Professional Research. Studies conducted by the international advisory bodies noted in the Introduction and by in-country policy staffs tend to concentrate on technical program features. Researchers in these organizations compile useful data on program provisions and frequently provide background information on the underlying economic and social factors that influence policy. The technical and training materials that originate in the ILO, ISSA, and OIP are used by analysts and policymakers throughout the world.

Numerous other international organizations contribute indispensable descriptive information on the level of development and program features of old-age pension schemes in both industrial and Third World nations. Because they lack money, staff, and time, however, these organizations conduct few comprehensive empirical or analytical research projects.

Cross-national studies seldom analyze the factors that underlie choices of one policy option over another or attempt to determine how various nations perceive, define, or measure the issues that affect the traits of programs targeted for the elderly population. While there are studies of the economic, social, and political conditions that confront social planners, there are only sporadic analyses of the elements that enter the decisionmaking process when planners contend with specific economic, social, and political conditions.

Some studies conducted by international organizations have limited applicability to comparative policy analysis, though their primary purpose is not comparative. For example, technical reports are published on financing, qualifying conditions, benefit levels, and the administration of social welfare programs. These reports are designed to help governments develop program features—often technical, administrative features—based on internationally accepted social insurance principles. They are not designed as a basis for cross-national comparison, though information that is marginally useful for such comparisons may be derived from them. Nor is current research designed to help policymakers understand why a specific strategy was adopted over all other choices or what other strategies were feasible. Perhaps most important, current studies do not provide comparative research models that would assist Third World planners in conducting their own investigations of other nations' programs and provisions.

PROCESS ANALYSIS IN CROSS-NATIONAL STUDIES

Comparative public policy studies first emerged as a subdiscipline of political science in the early 1970s (Heidenheimer, 1986; Hancock, 1983). As would be expected of a relatively new research discipline, a variety of conceptual frameworks were introduced during the 1970s and 1980s that were diverse in their "scope, emphasis, methods and findings" (Hancock, 1983:284). Researchers generally defined comparative public policy as "the cross-national study of how, why, and to what effect government policies are developed" (Heidenheimer, Heclo & Adams, 1975, cited in Hancock, 1983:284), and generally examined the influence of political parties, interest groups, and legislatures in order to determine relationships between variables and to build theory.

Comparative process analysis differs from public policy research models in several important ways, although it also hopes to arrive at "a better understanding of the making and implementation of public policy and of its effects" (Antal, Dierkes, & Weiler, 1987:17). First, it investigates the processes used in solving problems that are shared by several nations. Second, it examines the conditions under which a given strategy is chosen as a solution to a given problem and the consequences of choosing that strategy. Third, it uses a multidisciplinary approach, analyzing economic, political, and social determinants of the process.

In 1973 the British political scientist Richard Rose was the first to apply process analysis to cross-national research. He designed a linear model to demonstrate the dynamic relationships between a variety of political phenomena on policy in a cross-national context. Rose's framework sequentially analyzed 12 conditions:

1. the initial state in a society prior to public recognition that a policy need exists,

2. how policy issues are placed on the agenda of public controversy,

3. how demands are advanced,

4. the importance of the form of government for policy deliberations,

5. available resources and existing constraints,
6. the move toward a policy decision,
7. the determinants of governmental choice,
8. the context of the choice,
9. implementation,
10. the production of outputs,
11. policy evaluation, and
12. feedback.

Rose and others encouraged political scientists to view policymaking as a process, rather than a disjunctive decision, and to examine the stages in decisionmaking and policy formation—for example, policy initiation, implementation, operation, and impact (Jones, 1985).

The model used in this study has been strongly influenced by Rose's analytical prototype. It also borrows heavily from other paradigms in social work and political science that were not originally designed for cross-national research. Gill's framework for social policy analysis and synthesis, for instance, includes issue identification, policy objectives, implications for key processes, and factors affecting policy development and evaluation (Gill, 1976). These aspects have been incorporated into the model employed here. The model also draws on Robert Morris's typology for social policy analysis (1985), for its focus on the social norms that shape, constrict, and direct government action, and on the principles that guide a government as it meets new situations. It draws on Gilbert and Specht (1986), for its consideration of the benefit-allocation framework: what benefits are offered to whom, how are they delivered, and how are they financed.

The policy process model also owes a debt to Charles O. Jones's (1984) framework of government policy processes: problem definition, action, implementation, and evaluation. In addition, the model borrows from the analytical approach to social programs and social policy developed by Chambers (1986), which uses policy analysis to uncover information about policies that is of practical and applied value to decisionmakers. Finally, it utilizes the conceptual framework of the "most similar nation" model: instead of attempting to establish the universality of relationships, the "most similar nation" model is designed to enhance credibility of specific predictions about specific cases (Teune, 1978).

With few exceptions, frameworks for process analysis have been applied only in single-country studies. Elements of policy process analysis are sometimes integrated into other methodologies, but it is seldom the primary comparative tool, especially in studies of social policies in Third World nations. Instead, a normative framework, based on evaluative and advisory research procedures (MacPherson & Midgley, 1987), has been used to analyze social policy development in these nations. Evaluative research analyzes social policies and assesses their outcomes in terms of predefined criteria, attempting to determine the extent to which policy options meet declared goals and objectives. Advisory analysis is intended to "apply social policy knowledge for programmative purposes to establish social service provisions or to modify them" (MacPherson & Midgley, 1987:97). This method of analysis apprises policymakers of the procedures, technical aspects, and likely consequences of specific programs and provisions. It is produced by consultants in the ILO, WHO, ISSA, and the U.S. Agency for International Development (USAID). It also reflects the mission of various other national advisory bodies involved in social and economic development projects and programs in foreign nations.

The framework for policy analysis in this text is a modified advisory model; instead of being an instrument for improving technical procedures, it is designed to be a diagnostic tool for consultants and policymakers alike. It excludes evaluation material, even though such material is of value in policy research, because evaluation requires empirical data from on-site program investigation that is not within the purview of this study. The model does include an evaluation component as a desirable research element but not as an absolute requirement; even without evaluative information, policymakers can obtain sufficient information from the problem-solving process to make an informed decision about a particular program or policy.

A COMPARATIVE PROCESS ANALYSIS FRAMEWORK

Policymakers who are interested in program developments in other societies need comparative studies that are structured so that the findings have practical meaning. To find such a structure, analysts must pose two questions. First, what aspects of another country's program or provision do policymakers need to understand in order to judge its transferability? Second, what do they need to know about those aspects? To answer these questions satisfactorily, analysts need to help policymakers understand the process by which a particular provision was adopted and is being implemented. Then policymakers will know whether the identified issue or problem is comparable to the issue they face; what propelled the government into action; what obstacles had to be overcome to implement the provision; how the provisions fit into national social welfare policy goals; and what cost and resources the strategy entails?

If, for example, a nation has adopted a policy to promote occupational pensions or to raise the retirement age or to extend coverage to agricultural workers, what problem-solving process was involved in establishing the strategy? How are the strategies affected by limited resources, increasing numbers of elderly, urban migration, and declining family support? These questions are intended to determine how a provision is adopted and what it is meant to accomplish by isolating the policy issue and the distinctive strategies that are being employed.

The following is a more detailed discussion of each of the eight criteria of the comparative process model noted in the Introduction. The criteria shown in Chart 1 are explained below using policy issues relative to the elderly to illustrate how the model applies.

Government's Legal Responsibility for Social Welfare Policy

A first step in analyzing a program or provision in another nation is to acquire at least a basic awareness of the government's role in its development and its commitment to its successful implementation. This does not require an in-depth knowledge of the policymaking process but it does require information about government structure and the government's legal limits in intervention, including the extent to which it abides by these limits.

The government's authority in programs for the elderly can be measured by both the scope of its legal jurisdiction and its involvement in enforcing legislation. It is useful to know, for example, whether the government decisionmaking structure is centralized or decentralized and to what extent policies affecting the elderly are made at the federal, regional, or local level. Which government jurisdictions are responsible for the implementation and administration of programs?

Frequently there are discrepancies between constitutional or legal authority given to the national government and what takes place in actual practice. In some cases this is simply the result of constitutional laws that are beyond the fiscal or administrative capabilities of the government to implement. In other cases it may be the result of a deliberate policy decision by the government not to enforce the laws and declarations of previous governments. Knowledge of the presence of a variance between law and practice is of interest but is generally less important for analysis than information on how the government's role is actually operationalized in terms of program implementation. This requires an examination of the

Chart 1
A Policy Process Model of Comparative Analysis for
Examining Programs for the Elderly

    I.   Government's Legal Responsibility for Social Welfare
       A. Explains the national government's role in social policy in terms of legal or constitutional authority, responsibility and commitment.

    II. Government's Conceptual Orientation to Social Welfare
       A. Explains the government's role under one or more of five conceptual frameworks:
          1. Social insurance and social assistance
          2. Preventive and remedial programs
          3. Comprehensive and categorical programs
          4. Integrated and independent programs
          5. Public and private programs

    III. Obstacles to Government Intervention
       A. Analyzes the major obstacles to program implementation and performance that are identified by policymakers.
       B. Describes the different ways in which identified problems appear to affect policy and program decisions and strategies. Includes administrative, financial, geographic, staffing, political, and cultural constraints.

    IV. Catalyst for Government Intervention
       A. Explains what principal social, cultural, economic, and political factors are generally accepted as having contributed to legislative action that has already been taken. Explains which factors are generating demands for current action to address identified needs in spite of the obstacles to program development noted in section III.

V. Specific Needs Identified by Government
   A. Explains how the response to identified needs has been manifested, in terms of legislation, policy declarations, resource commitment, strategic decisions, and implementation.
   B. Describes the data base, if any, used in designating a specific program or provision as the appropriate strategy to address an identified need.

VI. Goals and Strategies
   A. Explains the general goals of a nation's approaches to identified needs as defined by the context of specific program provisions and objectives.
   B. Explains the acknowledged risks of specific strategies.
   C. Describes new or revised strategies, if any, being contemplated to address specific needs.

VII. Program Description
   A. Describes the major characteristics of the programs of each study country.
   B. Administration.
   C. Indicates which government unit, if any, is responsible for data collection. Indicates if general data are available.

VIII. Evaluation
   A. Assesses the impact that the policy, program, or provision has had in addressing the problem that was identified by the government and the objectives that were specified as a reason for the intervention.

IX. Analysis
   A. Synthesizes information.
   B. Provides implications of analysis for policy.
   C. Suggests specific needs for further research.

functions that are assumed by the national government in financing, administering, and delivering benefits.

Government's Conceptual Orientation to Social Welfare

Another important aspect of the national government's role and obligation is its conceptual orientation toward state involvement in social welfare policy. What are the predominant conceptual frameworks as gauged by government statements and legislative actions? This may be determined by inspecting programs in terms of contrasting policy orientation scales. For the purpose of analyzing programs for the elderly, the most explanatory measures of policy orientation are social insurance and social assistance, preventive and remedial, comprehensive and categorical, integrated and independent, and public and private. These are briefly explained below.

Social Insurance and Social Assistance. Much can be learned about a government's approach to meeting the needs of the elderly by examining its social insurance and social assistance programs. The level of commitment to either or both of these strategies helps to explain how the government perceives needs and its role in addressing them. The presence of social insurance programs can be interpreted to mean that the government accepts a measure of state obligation to protect individual wage earners and dependents from the exigencies of a wage-based economy. Whether the level of coverage and protection is significant or not, having social insurance programs in place suggests that the government accepts the concept that the state has a responsibility to make it possible for workers in covered employment to have a more financially secure old age. These programs are conceptualized as government-facilitated, but essentially worker-and employer-financed, systems of protecting against poverty and, in some cases, poor health as well.

Social assistance programs, in contrast, reflect the government's acknowledgement that certain impoverished individuals fall outside the protection of government social insurance and cannot rely on earnings-based support for adequate income or health care protection in old age. These are the uninsured elderly who, in many cases, constitute such a large proportion of the older population that national resources permit assistance to only the most deserving of the destitute. Definitions of those who "deserve" public assistance range from persons who have worked part time, or sporadically, in employment covered by social insurance to persons who simply demonstrate abject poverty.

Preventive and Remedial Programs. Another useful measure of how a government perceives its role in social programs is the degree of orientation toward prevention and remedial action. It is generally easier to finance and administer programs that are designed to react to symptoms of social and economic inequities. A system of income-tested benefits to indigent elderly agricultural workers, for example, is administratively less costly than a social insurance system. This is largely because an income-tested system avoids the enormous logistical problems involved in the process of collecting payroll taxes from rural workers and the difficulty of establishing eligibility and benefit levels for seasonal and nonwage-based workers.

At the same time, it is more cost-effective to provide social insurance for industrial workers in urban areas than to give them income-tested benefits. This is so because social insurance essentially pays for itself and income-tested benefits must come from general or special taxes. In addition, it is convincingly argued that social insurance stimulates economic growth through the availability of funds and increased consumer spending and, as Diessenbacher (1989) suggests, population control.

These fiscal and administrative advantages and disadvantages of adopting a preventive or remedial approach are well known to policymakers. Governments are never committed to one approach to the complete exclusion of another, but clear preferences do emerge upon analysis of policy statements and program provisions.

Such an analysis can be very useful in understanding the rationale for program strategies that are focused on raising income levels through employment and economic development. This is opposed to strategies that converge on ways to attempt to meet basic income, sanitation, food, and health needs that result from unemployment; or those that increase the responsibility of the family and community in helping the elderly play a greater social and economic role.

Comprehensive and Categorical Programs. Under the industrial model of social welfare, most needs are met by universal programs for the entire population of which the elderly are simply one segment. This is becoming less true for social services as well as certain health care programs that are targeted for elderly with special needs (i.e., frail elderly), but it remains an accurate description of the intent of the welfare state.

A universal approach to welfare is typically too expensive for most Third World nations. Nonetheless, many of these nations do aspire to provide at least a minimum coverage of basic needs and many are constitutionally committed to it. It is useful, then, to examine their programs and provisions in the context of meeting this goal because it often explains apparent anomalies in program strategies. For example, most Third World governments have agreed to the principle of providing primary health care for all by the year 2000 under the provisions of the 1978 Alma Ata conference. Clearly, however, most of these nations are not prepared to implement strategies to attain this goal that will address the basic health care needs of many elderly who suffer from chronic health problems to the exclusion of addressing the needs of the general population.

Integrated and Independent Programs. The magnitude of government involvement in programs for the elderly is also reflected by administrative structure. The government's ability to establish policy goals and implement programs may be conditioned by the historical evolution of one or several administrative agencies. Agencies may function independently from direct government control and may or may not complement the mission of related agencies. It is not unusual for several different branches of government to assume partial responsibility for program development. This affects how needs are defined and what strategies are seen as appropriate measures. Since it is common to find conflicting needs assessment and policy goals among agencies, the government's ability to intervene is often severely compromised.

Public and Private Programs. The role of the government is also dictated by the various factors that are pressuring governments to increase the involvement of the private sector in services and benefits for the elderly. This often helps to explain why certain government policies have been adopted that call for strategies that diminish the state's responsibility.

Obstacles to Government Intervention

A third step in analyzing government involvement in a comparative context is to investigate the major obstacles to policy development and program implementation. The purpose of this step is to identify factors that are perceived by government policymakers as barriers to government intervention. What are the most important variables that lead to caution or curtailment in government participation in programs for the elderly? These variables may be found among administrative, financial, geographic, staff, political, and cultural constraints. More specifically, obstacles to government intervention in programs for the elderly include a lack of financial resources, sizable rural populations, administrative deterrents, public resistance to government, public preference for the status quo, higher priority for other government programs, and burdensome numbers of informal workers. These impediments are discussed below.

Lack of Financial Resources. A foremost problem for both establishing new programs for the elderly and expanding old ones in Third World countries is the lack of financial resources. These resources for social programs have seriously deteriorated as national debts have risen to extraordinary proportions. For example, the national external debt as a percentage of gross national product in Costa Rica rose from 59.7% in 1980 to 126.3% in 1985. Comparable data over the same period in Argentina show an increase from 51.1% to 79.9%; in Turkey it rose from 33.5% to 49.2%; in Mexico from 31.9% to 58.3%; and in the Philippines from 49.6% to 80.6% (World Bank, 1987). This factor has been instrumental in generating support for social insurance systems that do not add to the nation's fiscal burden. Thus, policymakers look to programs that are self-funding and to private sector alternatives. This has led to policies that limit national programs to covering workers in industries where employees and employers can be taxed. It also has confined most government intervention targeted for the elderly to income programs, developing health care for the general population, and leaving social services to families and communities.

Administrative Deterrents. The problems of establishing an effective administrative organization can be overwhelming in nations where most of the population live in isolated rural areas. The difficulties of locating potential beneficiaries, taking applications, determining eligibility, adjudicating appeals, and paying benefits are exacerbated when there is only a small pool of properly trained staff, which is often the case. A related problem is that administrators must deal with populations with little formal education and limited literacy, especially among the elderly. This leads to complications in recipients' understanding qualifying conditions, application forms, and other entitlement procedures endemic of government programs.

Informal Workers. It has become commonplace in the urban areas of Third World nations for persons to earn a living by working in the informal work sector, relying on sales of products produced in cottage industries, odd jobs, and street enterprises. The extent of this phenomenon in Africa, for example, is estimated to be from 40% to 60% of the urban labor force (ILO, 1985). It is virtually impossible to structure contributory social insurance programs for these workers because there is no basis for determining entitlement or benefit amounts. The elderly who are most adversely affected by this barrier to benefits and services are women and persons who have been only marginally, if at all, employed for wages throughout their lives.

There is also a problem with implementing contributory social insurance programs in rural areas for seasonal, part-time, and nonwage earners who make up the plurality of agricultural workers. Again, women laborers are placed at unparalleled risk because they are most likely to fall in these categories of uninsured work.

Public Resistance to Government Involvement. National government involvement in the administration of public schemes that entail the collection and distribution of money is frequently viewed with suspicion and apprehension by workers and the public. It is not unusual, and not without reason, for the populace to distrust the competence of the government to maintain a stable environment capable of enforcing legislation. There is genuine concern that the government may not be able to maintain the fiscal integrity of a social insurance fund that will be capable of making payments to contributors during retirement. Not surprisingly, doubts about receiving a benefit fuel resistance to tax payments and payroll contributions.

A lack of confidence in the government also contributes to opposition to periodic pension payments in place of a lump-sum benefit. A lump-sum payment, such as that paid under provident fund systems and employment termination provisions, at least assures beneficiaries who reach retirement age that all the money owed to them is collected regardless of what happens to them or to the government. A periodic benefit, on the other hand, is paid in installments, usually monthly, and should the insurance system fail the benefits would cease.

Public Preference for the Status Quo. Meaningful changes of customary and traditional ways of doing things are difficult under the best of circumstances in any society. Change always involves trade-offs of gains and losses. When changing the status quo involves government intervention where before there was little or none, resistance can be quite strong. This is especially true if the government involvement threatens to invoke new authority or to impose new taxes.

Although formal government programs for the elderly are not as entrenched as those in industrial nations, there are firmly established traditional formal and informal systems in Third World nations in which many people have a vested interest. Proposals to change the way in which these systems function often threaten to undermine customs and practices that individuals expect to be in place when they reach old age. It can be very difficult to persuade individuals that a new government program will be equal to, or better than, the traditional means of support, even when the traditional means is not adequately addressing the needs of the elderly.

Priorities of Other Programs. The governments of Third World nations are faced with overwhelming service and structural needs, ranging from sanitation to employment for youth. The extreme shortages of income, food, housing, and health care for the general population, and especially children, is such that special programs for the elderly are sometimes viewed as a superfluous indulgence. While the needs of the elderly are beginning to be acknowledged, government policies often reflect a bias that the elderly would be best served by addressing the basic needs of the entire population. This view is particularly strong with regard to social services that have traditionally been provided by the family.

Priorities also play an important role with regard to bestowing greater importance on economic rather than social welfare development. Despite progress at the international level in gaining acceptance that social welfare is an integral part of effective development policies (United Nations, 1986a), social programs are still perceived as a secondary or residual goal to economic productivity and, often, defense. Government policies that give an exclusive priority to economic development are hard pressed to justify spending scarce resources on the elderly who are often perceived, however erroneously, as having little to contribute to the nation's productivity. In fact, they are often thought of as being a liability to economic development because they consume more than they produce and their personal beliefs and adaptive capacities are unfavorable to development (Treas & Logue, 1986).

Sources of Information on Obstacles. Information on the obstacles to government intervention in programs for the elderly is more difficult to obtain than descriptive data. However, studies that describe various programs often include at least a summarization of the variables that have played a historical role in preventing program development. These studies often analyze the rationales for program revisions and for new programs with an explanation of the most significant events that preceded the adoption of the legislation. While there is a tendency to focus on the elements that stimulated legislation, there may be some discussion of the factors that worked to restrict its scope.

Numerous documents and publications from government agencies are a valuable source of information on deterrents. While formal publications generated for widespread public consumption (i.e., annual yearbooks) typically restrict information to program features, less widely circulated documents are often more forward in assessing the problems involved in implementing programs. This type of more profound information is also found in the statements of government officials that are published in a variety of international journals and news sheets. Such documents are available in international repositories such as the resource facilities of the International Social Security Association and the International Labour Office in Geneva and the Social Security Administration's Office of International Policy in Washington, D.C.

Catalysts for Government Intervention

The purpose of this fourth phase in the process of analysis is to determine the social and economic forces that generate demands for government intervention in programs for the elderly. The step involves an exploration of the impact of the following variables: defining need, growing numbers and proportions of elderly, rural to urban migration of young people, diminishing

extended family support systems, a shift to a wage-based economy, increased longevity (especially for women after age 60),
earlier labor force withdrawal, increased labor force participation
of women (traditional care givers), rising poverty rates among
the elderly, national commitment to social solidarity, and national
commitment to government protection against exigencies of a
wage-based economy.

Changing Demographics. Many economically developing nations are just starting to experience the challenges to social policy
presented by aging populations. In the past, the elderly posed few
problems for Third World societies because they comprised a
small number of the population, they were generally cared for by
family members at home, and they were not a long-term family
burden because they usually died before reaching a very old age.
In recent years, however, these demographic and social patterns
have changed in very fundamental ways. The number of older
persons has grown dramatically in most Third World nations and
population projections forecast much greater increases in the near
future. Persons age 65 and over in the Third World will reach
470 million, more than double the number in developed nations,
by the year 2020 (Kinsella, 1988). The number of elderly in
almost all Third World nations still constitutes a small proportion
of the population. They generally have less than a proportion of
7%, which is the accepted yardstick of an elderly population
(Chow, 1989), but the rate of increase is escalating at a time when
there are fewer financial resources to address their income,
health, and social service needs.

Traditional Family Support. Moreover, traditional sources of
family support have begun to wane under the advent of industrialization and wage-based economies. The ability of families to
care for the elderly has diminished as extended families become
more nuclear (Midgley, 1984a; Pistirio, 1985); as young people
migrate from rural to urban areas leaving their parents behind
(Sykes & Sykes, 1986); as fewer children are born due to family
planning measures; as housing space becomes more restrictive,
leaving no room for parents and grandparents; and as women who

once were caretakers become employed, leaving the elderly without daily in-home support. The problems confronting family care are compounded by a rising number of women, especially widows, who live into very old age. Many older women live by themselves, have a meager income, and suffer from chronic health diseases (Gibson, 1985).

Poverty. These conditions have attracted the attention of Third World policymakers and social welfare advocates for several associated reasons. In the first place, there is the patently obvious abject need of many elderly for income and support services. That is, the elderly have begun to swell the ranks of the impoverished and have become much more publicly visible than in the past. Second, the extent of poverty among the elderly has made it apparent that the traditional systems of support are unable to effectively meet the needs of the growing numbers of older persons. This situation is worsened by an increasing frequency of poverty among adult children, who may themselves be old and in need of care, but also have the burden of providing support for their parents.

Pressure for Government Action. The fundamental, and often constitutional, commitment of governments to the principle of protection against wage-related risks of loss of income has put acute political pressure on national legislatures and bureaucracies to respond to the increasing income needs of a growing number of older persons. The pressure, much of it exerted by workers and trade unions, challenges the efficacy of the current status of programs for the elderly, particularly old-age insurance pension programs. It also raises critical policy issues regarding the appropriate respective roles of national and local government, family, community, employers, and private insurance in addressing the income needs of indigent elderly persons.

In addition, there is pressure for governments to review specific program features such as funding, qualifying conditions, benefit levels, and program administration. Social services and health care delivery systems targeted for the elderly are, as well, being examined by policymakers in light of changing demographic and social conditions. However, with regard to their application to older persons as distinct from the rest of the population, these services are clearly perceived by governments as a subordinate priority to income maintenance program development.

Social Solidarity. Finally and, perhaps, most importantly, policymakers are concerned about the rise in the incidence of elderly people because of the threat to income security for both workers and nonworkers in retirement age. The governments of many nations, including economically developing ones, have adopted formal legal commitments to protect workers and their dependents from the risk of lost income due to contingencies associated with wage-based economies, including work accidents, sickness, maternity, disability, redundancy (unemployment), and old age. A shortage of fiscal resources in Third World countries has typically resulted in incremental introductions of programs covering these exigencies, but they are obligated to them in principle if not always in practice.

Specific Needs

The fifth analytical stage is concerned with how a government identifies its need for involvement in the delivery of programs and services and defines the form of intervention it will take. Knowledge of what the government perceives to be important or a priority is of obvious value in understanding the characteristics of specific programs and provisions.

Definition of Need. Defining and assessing the needs of the elderly is elusive because accurate empirical data are difficult to obtain under the best of research conditions. This means that policymakers in the Third World, as well as advisors from international agencies, must often make goals and develop strategies without the benefit of complete or reliable data. Although data are limited, most policy decisions are based on whatever information is at hand, including subjective as well as objective research, reports, anecdotes, personal impressions, and biases of individuals inside and outside of government.

The point is that the decision to act or not to act, to choose a single strategy or a set of strategies over all other possibilities is based on criteria that, if known, would be instrumental in understanding the government's position on any policy affecting the elderly. The policy, moreover, may not even be based on documented need but, rather, on government policy priorities that may or may not be supportive of programs for the elderly. A decision to raise the retirement age for old-age pensions, for example, may be due to actuarial projections that the pension scheme will become bankrupt if such action is not taken. However, the decision may result from a shortage of skilled manpower that threatens national interests with scant regard for the impact on the individual worker. Either explanation has important implications for analysts from another nation who want to understand why the study country raised the retirement age to see if a similar action is suitable to address their own policy concerns.

Obtaining Data. The factors that actually influence a policy decision are difficult to obtain. It is rare to find published documentation of the informal decisionmaking process involved in setting goals and strategies. Formal rationales for policy decisions, however, are available when a new or revised program or provision is openly debated in the legislature. Informative materials on the reasons for legislative action, or the lack of it, are contained in various legislative documents such as first and second readings, commission reports, published planning documents (i.e., five-year plans), journal articles, newspaper commentaries, and academic papers. Most of these materials are published only in the local language and many are not kept in foreign libraries and resource facilities. The major exception is the resource facilities of the Social Security Administration and the ISSA.

Goals and Strategies

After information is obtained on the government's perception of need, a sixth stage in the analysis determines the goals that are set to address the need and the specific strategies that are implemented to achieve the goals. This includes an examination of the long- and short-term goals, strategies, the trade-offs involved in strategies, and strategies under discussion.

Long- and Short-Term Goals. It is useful to differentiate between long- and short-term goals in order to accurately assess the purpose of the program or provision under scrutiny. A common short-term objective, for example, is to provide old-age pension protection for employed persons in urban areas while a long-term goal is to expand coverage to the general population.

Strategies. Each general goal and operationally defined objective must have some programmatic means of implementation or strategy. The strategies may, in fact, be of most interest to policymakers because they reveal the specific action upon which the government is relying to address the area of identified need within the nation's economic, political, social, and cultural constraints.

Risks of Strategies. It is necessary, however, to know not only what the strategies are but the risks, or potential benefit trade-offs, that are involved in their use. For example, low benefit levels or negligible services that are employed as a strategic approach to control program expenditures may diminish public support and ultimately prevent attainment of long-term goals. Adopting pay-as-you-go financing may be an ill-advised strategy if circumstances prevent the fund from meeting its contractual obligations. Raising contribution rates under the public pension scheme in order to extend coverage may have a deleterious effect on employers' interest and ability to develop employer-sponsored pension plans. Extending social insurance coverage for income or health benefits may threaten the continued existence of other forms of retirement benefits, such as termination pay and severance pay. Benefits that are targeted to special populations may raise opposition that can question the value and desirability of entire programs.

New Strategies. Finally, it is useful to know as much as possible about new and revised strategies that are being considered to address specific issues and identified needs.

Program Description

An essential seventh step in analyzing programs for the elderly in a cross-national context is to accumulate information on the basic provisions of the enabling legislation. This includes a description of who gets what, when, and how. Answers to these questions provide information on the rules and regulations for entitlement, the type of benefit available (periodic, lump sum), benefit amounts (as a percent of a standard index), and the application process (including publicity efforts to reach all entitled persons). The description should also reveal how the program is financed (contributions, general contributions, earmarked taxes, mixture of several mechanisms). Also of value is information on how the program is administered and the status of data collection.

This type of information is available in a variety of publications. The most inclusive of these are *Social Security Programs Throughout the World,* produced biennially by the U.S. Social Security Administration, and the *International Social Security Review,* published quarterly by the ISSA. Briefly stated legislative developments are readily found in the International Labor Organization's *Social and Labour Bulletin.*

Other widely distributed published sources of descriptive program information include: *Ageing International, Benefits & Compensation International, Employee Benefits Plan Review, International Labour Review,* and *Labour and Society.*

Administration. An important aspect in describing the basic features of the system is information on how it is administered. This would include an explanation of the agency or agencies responsible for the program under study and what role they play in initiating legislation and in formulating rules, regulations, and procedures.

Data Collection. It is useful to know not only who within the government is responsible for collecting data on particular programs, but also what data are collected. Ideally, information should be obtained on how the data are collected and aggregated so that their comparability can be ascertained.

Evaluation

The eighth element is that of evaluation. This provides information on the impact of the program or provision in terms of the original goals and objectives. It includes information on the consequences of the strategy on the target population, including any unanticipated effects. Evaluation should also examine indirect and direct costs. As noted, a thorough evaluative analysis would require in-depth data that are generally not available, but cursory evaluations can usually be made based on more general knowledge of goals and outcomes that are of value.

Analysis

There are three discussion areas that make up the ninth task in the analytical framework. These include a synthesis of the information that has been obtained from the seven basic steps; a discussion of the possible application or transferability of policies, programs, and provisions in other nations; and suggestions for additional research.

SUMMARY

This text offers a model for cross-national analysis of social and health programs for the elderly, especially old-age pension systems, in Third World nations. The value of building theoretical knowledge, of increasing understanding of macro social, economic, and political variables, and of providing technical support is recognized and encouraged. But, the case is made that such studies are limited in meeting many of the practical informational needs of national program planners who are faced with making decisions about the appropriateness of various provisions. It is suggested that an approach to making better informed decisions is to analyze the process that underlies program strategies in other countries used to respond to similar demographic, employment, and social issues of problem definition, needs assessment, goal setting, objective specification, legislative and regulative formulation, program implementation, administration, and evaluation.

It is important to note that the task of gathering information is not bound by any particular order of investigation. Much of the information required of this model must be obtained from documents, publications, and unpublished materials that do not necessarily directly address the questions posed by the model. Thus it is often necessary to extract small segments of pertinent information from materials that have been prepared for quite different purposes. It is imperative, then, that the analyst examine these materials with the objective of procuring any information that may pertain to any of the model's nine steps of inquiry. It is also important to recognize that analysis may not be best served by addressing the questions in the order in which they are presented in Chart 1. Peculiarities of historical welfare program development and current conditions may require the analyst to deviate from the order. The content is more important than the sequence in which it is obtained or discussed.

STUDY COUNTRIES

This volume uses case presentations of examples in four nations and a state in a fifth country to illustrate various applications of the methodology—the Peoples' Republic of China, Kerala (a state in southern India), Mexico, Nigeria, and Turkey. An outline of the policy process model used in the text is given in Chart 1.

The study nations were chosen for analysis on the basis of their relatively comparable levels of economic development but yet diverse representation of a spectrum of programs, political systems, cultures, and geographic descriptions. They were also selected because of unique program features that are of value to professionals and students interested in how other nations are

responding to similar demographic, social, and economic pressures.

The People's Republic of China provides an opportunity to
examine the policies of a nation that does not have centralized
comprehensive programs for the elderly but, rather, has relied
on locally administered efforts. Retirement benefits, for example,
are the responsibility of local- and state-run enterprises that
assume full responsibility for funding and paying pensions. Social
services and health care are similarly provided under a decentralized structure. The state of Kerala in India has had an innovative
income-tested pension program for indigent male and female
agricultural workers in place since 1980, which may be applicable
in various Third World settings.

Policies in Mexico are of special interest because of the Latin
and South American traditions of strong constitutional commitment to programs for the elderly. Mexico is dedicated to expanding coverage to its rural workers, which is of interest to other
nations seeking to expand coverage to rural areas. Mexican
government policies have enabled the country to develop an
extensive social security infrastructure that nevertheless, is encumbered with obstacles that are important to assess.

Nigeria was chosen for study because it represents a nation
whose government has had little pressure to react to issues
concerning its aging population. It is of special interest because
of the significance to traditional support systems for the elderly
that follow from a modicum of direct government involvement.
The Turkish experience with increasing numbers of elderly is of
interest because of its high levels of old-age pension coverage and
entitlement, including certain agricultural workers, in a youth-
dominated society.

3

The People's Republic of China: Decentralized Government Programs for the Elderly

As in most other economically developing nations, more government attention is being paid to the elderly in the People's Republic of China (PRC) because of identified needs that have accompanied urbanization, the impact of family planning policies, the nuclearization of families, increased longevity, and escalating proportions of older persons. Government policy decisions and program strategies regarding income, health care, and social services for the elderly conform to national goals of administrative decentralization accompanied by strengthening the role of families and community.

It is only very recently that the government has had to concern itself at all with the care of the elderly. As a result, formalized public social service, health, and income maintenance programs designed for this population are in the early stages of formation. In the past, there was a virtually exclusive reliance on informal family and community support systems that were based on a high esteem for older persons that is deeply ingrained in the nation's social fabric. Current policies continue to reflect a heavy dependence on local support and high regard for the elderly.

The decentralized administrative system, which contrasts with the conceptual framework of unified government control when the Communist government first assumed power in 1949, reflects an attempt to give more authority to community officials so that programs may be better adapted to local conditions. Under this process, the central government sets policies and guidelines but depends on local state-owned enterprises, communities, and cadres to administer them according to community resources and needs. Even pension programs, which are essentially limited to urban areas, are funded and managed by local state enterprises and production units rather than by the central government (see Chart 2).

An aspect that has been instrumental in shaping programs for the elderly since the Communist revolution in 1949 is the conviction that the nation's socioeconomic structure depends as much on the elderly to contribute to the family and community as it does on the family and community to support the elderly (Sher, 1984). The notion of retirement in the PRC typically signals the beginning of a new mode of contribution rather than the onset of leisure. Leaving wage-based employment is viewed as a transition from one socially and economically useful role to another that is equally valuable (Dixon, 1981; Sher, 1984). Most elderly assume household chores, work in small businesses, and become active in civic affairs.

In the rural areas, where 80% of the population resides, the principal means of support for the elderly is a combination of employment and dependence on married sons (Tang, 1989; Davis-Friedmann, 1985). When the family is incapable, or there is no family, the community and local government (often in the form of production teams) are required to ensure the "Five Guarantees" (*Wu-bao Hu*) of food (including fuel, cooking utensils, pocket money), shelter, clothing, medical care, and burial expenses to the needy (Mok, 1983; Dixon, 1985; Barnes, 1987; Chuanyi, 1989). The standard of living under the system of Wu-bao Hu must be equal to that of the average living standard of the society in which the recipient lives (Tang, 1989).

About 75% of the total work force depends on the family for care in old age but they are also beneficiaries of legal mandates that require the collective or commune to provide personal social services or income allowances (Dixon, 1985). This provides a

Chart 2
Old-Age Pension Provisions in the People's
Republic of China

The basic provisions for entitlement to old-age benefits are under the Labour Insurance Regulations as briefly outlined below. For a more complete description of the pension system in the PRC, see Lillian Liu's chapter on "Social Insurance in China" in the *International Handbook on Social Insurance* (Tracy & Pampel, 1991).

Coverage. Employed persons in state-run enterprises and contract workers are covered under the 1978 "Provisional Procedures for Worker's Retirement and Disability." Civil servants are covered under separate schemes. Rural workers who do not qualify for a pension are entitled to protection under the Five Guarantees provided by the community.

Qualifying conditions. A worker must be continuously employed in the same enterprise for at least 10 years. Retirement age is 60 for men, 55 for women white-collar workers, and 50 for blue-collar employees. Retirement is mandatory. Workers in arduous employment can receive a pension up to five years earlier.

Benefit formula. The basic pension amount is 60% of the last month's standard wage. If the worker has 15 to 20 years of continuous employment, the amount is raised to 70% and to 75% for 20 years or more. Additional amounts are awarded to model workers or revolutionary heroes. There is a minimum monthly benefit amount of 30 yuan (in 1987).

Financing. The state enterprise pays the entire cost of pensions for its retirees out of its operating budget under the guidance of special committees. Benefits for contract workers are funded by an employee contribution of 3% of wages and an employer contribution of 15% of payroll.

Administration. The Ministry of Labor and Personnel establishes general policies and guidelines but each state enterprise administers its pension program under the supervision of local government and party cadres.

major safety net provision in the PRC and, indicative of such assistance programs, is essentially a means-tested benefit.

Care of the elderly in the PRC, then, is still essentially a responsibility of the family and community bolstered by public programs for health care and by a variety of means-tested social assistance provisions for social services and income maintenance. The efficacy of this approach, however, is under increasing scrutiny as it becomes more apparent that changing social and demographic conditions create a need that requires further government program assessment and planning (Chow, 1989).

The central questions addressed here are how government planners and policymakers have responded to a perceived need for intervention and what factors have functioned either to advance or impede their involvement in developing programs for the elderly.

FACTORS THAT RESTRICT NATIONAL PROGRAM DEVELOPMENT

There are various identifiable factors that help to explain why comprehensive national social service and income maintenance programs for the elderly have been slow to evolve in the PRC. Foremost among these are the tradition of filial piety, dilemmas over policies relative to a burgeoning population, insufficient economic resources, widespread illiteracy in rural areas, resistance to pension expansion, and a reliance on family and community care.

Filial Piety

A major constraint in the development of public programs to aid the elderly is the presence of the strong sense of filial piety, which places the obligation of care of the elderly on the family, especially the sons. Filial piety has been an exceptional force in China for thousands of years as a major tenet of Confucianism, Buddhism, and folk religions (Sher, 1984). Over the years, the elderly maintained a position of great economic and political power by virtue of their control over inheritance rights. Much of the source of these powers was removed by the Communist revolution in 1949, which eliminated laws of primogeniture and distributed land to various age groups. Moreover, it has been suggested that the belief that the elderly are held in respect in Chinese societies is much less of a factor than is generally thought (Chow, 1989).

Official party attitudes toward the elderly went through a brief period of ambivalence in the early 1950s following the revolution. On the one hand, the Communist Party wanted to deemphasize filial piety in order to promote a greater sense of responsibility among young people to society as a whole. Apparently there was some early overexuberance in instigating this policy with the undesirable result of a notable increase in the incidence of elder abuse, neglect, and homelessness (Dixon, 1981).

On the other hand, official policy clearly obligated the family as responsible for the well-being of the elderly, as put forth in the Marriage Law of 1950 (Article 49 of the new constitution), which states that "children who have come of age have the duty to support and assist their parents" (Sher, 1984). If the children have died, the obligation conveys to the grandchildren (Tout, 1989). This policy is in accord with the national government's efforts to decentralize responsibility for most social programs. Under current law, if children do not fulfill their obligation to their parents, the parents can appeal to the childrens' place of employment and have part of their pay garnished. In rural areas where children may be employed in nonwage work activity, parents have a legal claim on part of their children's commercial grain ration (Petri, 1982). There is a penalty of up to five years of imprisonment for flagrant noncompliance (Tout, 1989).

Population Crisis

Also working against the development of government programs for the elderly is the concern over a critical population predicament. China has over 1.1 billion people (in 1988), which is one-fifth of the world's population. With only 7% of the land suitable for agricultual production, the government has projected that it can support only

1.2 billion people. A government response to this situation in the early 1970s was an intense family planning program to control the rate of population growth. The program began in 1971 and evolved into a one-child policy campaign in 1979 for families in urban areas. In rural areas two children are permitted in many cases, especially if the first child is a girl (Chuanyi, 1990). Although family planning is a reasonable priority, it creates a policy dilemma for the government with regard to the elderly. The fewer young people that are born, the fewer there will be to support the elderly. Moreover, since care of the elderly is supposed to be provided by the son, in cases of one-child only, half of the elderly will be without the assistance of children as half of the children are girls (Liang, Chuanyi & Jihui, 1985).

A decline in birth rates is of paramount importance as children have long been relied upon as the caregivers and providers for elderly persons who can no longer provide for themselves. Not only are there fewer or no siblings to share in the care of elderly parents, the family also loses prospective uncles, aunts, and other relatives who traditionally make up the extended family network (Liang, Chuanyi & Jihui, 1985).

Thus, the success of the family planning creates a complex situation for the state (Chow, 1988). This works to both hamper and foster government programs to assist the elderly. It impedes programs because people are resistive to the idea of giving up a way of life that has been practiced for generations. It boosts programs because once the society has acquiesced to a policy of one child, government programs must assume some of the burden of care as a viable substitute to the family and community.

Studies have shown that women are more inclined to support family planning if there is some assurance of pension and social service benefits (Liang, Chuanyi & Jihui, 1985).

Limited Economic Resources

Another impediment to program development is the spending restrictions imposed by China's low per capita gross national product (GNP), which is ranked in the bottom third of developing countries. The absence of available funds makes it difficult to finance programs for the elderly on a national basis. While a case can be made that a national scheme such as a social insurance pension system actually contributes to economic growth, it does not appear that this argument has been a convincing one among policy planners in the PRC.

Limited resources inevitably generate government interest in programs that are income-tested or means-tested. This allows the government greater control over expenditures by focusing only on those who are at extreme risk. Such programs are also attractive to the government because they can be more easily administered and funded.

Illiteracy

Program development is also encumbered by the prevalence of an illiterate population, especially in the rural areas. About 80% of the people continue to live and work in rural areas where the illiteracy or semi-illiteracy rate is 82% (Liang, Chuanyi & Jihui, 1985). Both factors work against the feasibility of centralized social insurance and social service programs that require trained personnel at the local level to implement and manage programs. Moreover, a social insurance system cannot function properly unless workers understand their rights and obligations, which generally requires a certain level of literacy. There are also the overwhelming difficulties of financing and administering programs in rural areas as discussed in the book's introduction.

Changes in Pensions of Covered Workers

An impediment to expanding coverage of old-age pension programs that are in place in the PRC is the resistance of urban workers who are already protected by a system that is entirely financed by employers (Chow, 1988). It is not uncommon for protected workers to view proposed changes in government programs with great suspicion. This is particulary true when proposals allude to the possibilty of introducing payroll contributions to finance pensions because it would reduce their net pay.

The influence of covered workers seems to be relatively strong despite the fact that apparently only a small proportion of wage earners work in covered employment (about 23% of the civilian labor force in 1985) (Liu, 1991). The source of their strength is that they tend to be educated, vocal, and represented by well-organized trade unions. In addition, certain influential civil servants are also entitled under a social insurance program. Although theirs is a separate program from that for wage earners, changes in pension program structures at the national level could also threaten their system with revisions that may generate anxiety.

One other important factor that has contributed to the slow progression of an old-age pension system based on the social insurance model was the Cultural Revolution of 1965–76. This delayed development because pensions were regarded as capitalistic and retirement was anti-socialist (Liu, 1991).

Family and Community Care

As noted, a sense that the family and community have the major responsibility of caring for the elderly permeates government policy decisions. There is a general assumption, however unfounded it may be, that the elderly are essentially abandoned by families in Western socities and that extensive national government programs of social insurance have contributed to this unfavorable situation. In the PRC, dependence on family, community, employers, and, in urban areas, local pension programs is sanctioned by the government as a means of lessening the need for institutionalized care of the elderly.

There is recognition that health and social services are necessary to keep the elderly well and active and there are apparently readily available services for needy elderly at the local level. Elderly residents receive regular counseling and home visits by cadres from the retirees' trade union former work unit and domiciliary services are provided to those who need them, including home nursing, home help, and companionship (Dixon, 1981). There seems to be a general acceptance that this is a local responsibility that can best be dealt with by the family and community within broad national guidelines. Although there are no formal assessments as to the effectiveness of the residential services, informal obserververations suggest that they do cater to the needs of the old (Hui, 1987).

The emphasis on family and community resources has limited development of long-term care facilities. In 1984, only 0.33% of the population aged 65 and over were in public insitutions (Liang, Chuanyi & Jihui, 1985). Nevertheless, as the population of persons aged 75 and over expands, accompanied by a growth in the incidence of debilitating conditions associated with the very old, there has been a steady increase, albeit small, in the number of long-term care facilities. They remain, however, primarily to provide services for elderly who have neither family or income (Baihua, 1987).

FACTORS THAT FOSTER GOVERNMENT INTERVENTION

In contradistinction to the various factors that have impeded the development of public social programs for the elderly in the PRC, there are a variety of demographic and social conditions that have compelled the government to become more involved in program decisions and coping strategies.

Demographic Changes

The aging of the Chinese population is a critical element contributing to recent discussions in government ministries about the respective roles of the family, community, and national government in providing for the needs of the elderly. A significant number of elderly persons has an obvious impact on government planning and budgeting and in the PRC the 65 and over population reached 59.8 million in 1988 and could rise to 175.7 million by 2020 (Kinsella, 1988). At this rate, the proportion of the population aged 65 and over will increase from 5.5% in 1988 to 8.1% by the year 2005. The proportion of persons aged 55 and over will rise from 12.2% in 1988 to 16.0% in 2005. As in many other nations, it is improved health conditions and medical care that have led to increased longevity, but these pose new problems for policymakers.

Coinciding with the growth in the number of older persons, the quantity of people who are retired is projected to rise from about 14 million in 1985 to 40 million by 2000 (Ministry of Labor and Personnel, 1986). This will present a major funding problem for the national government, which increased expenditures on programs for the elderly from 0.5% of the GNP in 1978 to 1.8% in 1985 (Liu, 1991). The likelihood of higher program costs puts considerable pressure on the government to devise ways and means to address the health, social, and income needs of this population. Although the preferred approach is to generate programs that will strengthen the family's ability to care for elderly members, it is increasingly recognized that government programs will have to assume a greater direct role, particularly in the area of old-age pensions.

The combined effect of these demographic changes and government interest in ways to address the changes has led to the emergence of government-sanctioned public and academic organizations such as the China National Aging Studies Committee formed in 1981 and the China Gerontological Committee established in 1983, spawning numerous branch committees at the local level. An important aspect of these types of organizations is that they promote research and data gathering that can be used by policymakers and planners. Information obtained by these committees is very likely to be used in the five-year plans at the regional and city level that have begun to include goals and objectives for the elderly (Liang, Chuanyi & Jihui, 1985).

Public and academic interest in the elderly is also indicated by the growth of the number of journals that focus on gerontology and by the large volume of volunteer groups of young persons who have emerged in recent years (Programmes for China's 80 Million Elderly, 1984).

Planned Economy

Another element that contributes to greater government involvement in programs affecting the elderly is the PRC's commitment to a planned economy. A vital feature of this approach to economic development is for the central government to assume responsibility for the economic well-being of workers, especially urban workers. Income, social services, and health care in retirement are specifically cited as important aspects of this responsibility (Liu, 1991). At the very least, the inclusion of retirement policies in national five-year plans indicates an awareness by the national government of the need to respond to social and demographic changes.

Urban Elderly

Pressure for policymakers to seek ways to improve pension and social service programs in urban areas descends from undeniable larger proportions of elderly in these areas. One reason that a significant proportion of retired people live in urban areas is a result of strict restrictions on migration of young people from villages to cities (Liang, Chuanyi & Jihui, 1985). Previously, the government response to the needs of the urban elderly had been to ask the industrial state enterprises to provide pensions and social services for their retired workers.

The burden placed on state enterprises to provide pensions and fringe benefits to retirees, however, has become excessive in industries that are old. This has led to a new strategy to pool the resources of all state enterprises in catchment areas so that the younger industries can share the load of paying for benefits for retired workers. Some 87% of the cities and counties now participate in resource pooling for labor insurance (Liu, 1991).

Nuclear Family Units

An additional impetus for increased government intervention in providing social benefits for the elderly is the attenuation of the extended family system (Chuanyi, 1989) and the subsequent increase in nuclear family arrangements. There is some question as to whether this has occurred in fact or only in attitude. One well-respected scholar suggests that the extent of relatives in family living arrangements beyond the parents and the children tends to be exaggerated and that the composition of families has not changed much in modern times (Pye, 1984). One reason is that high mortality rates means that relatively few elderly survive long enough to live in a household with multiple generations (Tu, Liang & Li, 1989). An additional cause of a rising number of nuclear families is related to the desire of young persons to live in small family units in urban areas because of limited housing space and because working couples can support themselves without assistance from the elderly (Sher, 1984).

Government Communes

The need for greater central government intervention in the care of the elderly has also accompanied the decline of the commune since the early 1980s. Formerly funds for services for the needy, including the elderly, were obtained by a deduction from the produce of commune production brigades. Now production brigades have difficulty enforcing this tax, as peasants are responsible for their own land. Thus, much of the burden has shifted to the Ministry of Civil Affairs, which is responsible for the social security system but has not yet been able to make up the loss of commune generated revenue (Chow, 1988).

Mandatory Retirement

Mandatory retirement provisions have been strictly enforced since 1986 in the PRC (Tang, 1989) in an effort to reduce the high unemployment rate among young people. The policy, similar to that of several European nations, is based on the assumption that getting older workers out of the formal labor force will open up job opportunities for younger workers. One measure to ensure that job replacement does occur is the "dingti" system. Under this scheme, workers in state enterprises who are age 55 and over can retire early if their adult child replaces them.

At the same time, it is not expected that a retired worker will necessarily enter a life of leisure. As noted, the elderly are expected to play an important role in community, commerce, and civic work. Older persons often assume important community positions as arbitrators and planners. In addition, many elderly women accept the role of taking care of grandchildren and the home while their adult children work. Other elderly sell agricultural products in small stalls or work in small industries and businesses at the village level (Tang, 1989).

SPECIFICALLY DESIGNATED NEEDS

The social and demographic conditions that have brought attention to the needs of the elderly have resulted in specifically designated areas of concern that government officials have targeted for resolution. The areas under discussion include administrating programs for the elderly, revising the old-age pension benefit formulae, and reducing the pension burden on state enterprises.

Administration

One recently released analysis by the the Research Unit of the Ministry of Civil Affairs identified the following as specific problem areas in the current approach to programs for the elderly:

(1) a lack of coordination among administrative units, (2) insurance programs are not flexible enough to respond to needs emanating from economic reforms, (3) excessive reliance on state funding, and (4) the development of social welfare and assistance is behind that of income (Ministry of Labor and Personnel, 1986).

Pension Benefit Formula

The currently used method of calculating benefit levels of old-age pensions in state enterprises has also come under criticism. The benefit formula is based on a progressively higher replacement rate of the last month's standard wage. Workers receive from 60 to 75% of the standard wage according to their length of work in covered employment ranging from 10 to 20 years. This is viewed as inequitable for persons with more than 20 years of covered work. In addition, the benefit formula does not incorporate "floating" wages, which are paid as a regular bonus to most workers. Thus, the replacement rate is not based on actual preretirement income. A third very important criticism of the current method of benefit calculation is that there is no provision for adjusting benefits to inflation (Ministry of Labor and Personnel, 1986).

State Enterprise Retirement Obligations

The government would also like to reduce the burden on state enterprises that may be providing retirement benefits to as many as 50% of their current work force (Tang, 1989). This is a situation that has obvious adverse consequences on the level of resources available to the enterprise for reinvestment and development. An apparent attempt to avoid this situation in newly formed private enterprises is to allow them not to provide pension benefits comparable to state-run industries (Xia, 1987).

GOALS AND STRATEGIES

Both the indistinct and more precisely identified issue areas noted above have resulted in miscellaneous short- and long-term goals and strategies that are at varying stages of discussion. Among those being given greatest consideration are the possibility of expanding pension coverage to agricultural workers, encouraging older persons to leave the formal labor market prematurely, experimenting with locally managed social insurance schemes, introducing pension schemes that are funded by variable contribution rates based on geographic location, and implementing mutual assistance funds.

Expand Program Coverage

A major long-term goal concerning the elderly is to provide adequate services, health care, and pensions without diminishing the role of the family and without centralized government management. Further, it is hoped that coverage can be extended to all workers in private enterprises, contract workers (workers employed by state enterprises for a specific period of time), and agricultural workers (Liang, Chuanyi & Jihui, 1985). As mentioned above, the basic approach has been to delegate pension funding and administrative responsibility to local state enterprises. A criticism of this practice is the difficulty it presents in maintaining equity among geographic areas with diverse economic resources (Pye, 1984).

The decentralization of pensions has met with considerable difficulty in that state enterprises cannot adequately contend with the fiscal obligations of caring for a large number of retirees (Ministry of Labor and Personnel, 1986). Moreover, the method impedes labor mobility, which is a high priority, as there is no vesting or transferring of accumulated retirement benefits from one industry to another. Thus, workers who move lose whatever they have contributed to their pension system (Liu, 1991).

Consequently, while there is a desire to decentralize the implementation and management of programs, there is counter-pressure to centralize the system into a state operated social insurance program. Additional incentives toward centralization have resulted from recent recommendations of a 1985 World Bank study that favor a compulsory national old-age pension system (Chow, 1988). Despite such pressure, strategies that are being explored fall short of a national scheme. A proposal by the Ministry of Labor and Personnel, for example, is to gradually introduce pension funds at the local level in municipalities and counties ("China Faces Problems in Social Security," 1987). This ministry has responsibility to admininister and reform the pension and social security system for urban workers. Its approach is to expand coverage on a step-by-step basis to urban workers in each province and then to implement the program nationwide at some unspecified later date.

A somewhat different strategy being considered by the Ministry of Civil Affairs, which is responsible for social security program development in rural areas and for peasants, is promoting the integration of different insurance schemes with existing welfare services rather than developing a single, unified system. This system would be funded primarily from the enterprise with contributions from the state and employees (DeLisle, 1989).

Early Retirement

One immediate pension policy objective is to open up employment positions for younger workers by easing older workers out of the wage-based labor market. In addition to mandatory retirement, there is a recent attempt to make retirement more attractive by relaxing qualifying conditions, raising benefit levels, and adding new grants and subsidies (Liu, 1991). It is important to note that this emphasis is not designed to negate the prevailing expectancy of older persons to continue working in other than wage-based employment.

Locally Managed Social Insurance Funds

Another short-term policy objective has been to encourage the development of locally managed social insurance programs in several large urban areas. These programs use local insurance carriers that accept contributions from collective enterprises based on a fixed percentage of payroll. The carrier sets aside the funds and guarantees benefits (Chow, 1988). This reduces much of the risk associated with pension funds operated by state enterprises, which may not be fiscally solvent when the worker reaches retirement age. About 10,000 towns with 3 million beneficiaries currently participate in these programs (Chuanyi, 1989).

Mutual Assistance Funds

A form of social assistance income protection plans that have emerged in moderately developed areas, primarily in Jiangxi Province, are Mutual Assistance Funds (MAF). These funds provide grants and loans for a variety of services, including medical care and pensions, to qualified persons who meet a means test. They are financed by contributions of 1% to 2% of the personal income of farmers and workers and total revenues of industrial and agricultural production (Chuanyi, 1989).

About 4 million households are covered under some 19,000 plans. The programs' popularity stems from the traditional Chinese emphasis on mutual assistance and the current official endorsement of local, democratic management of public welfare services and income maintenance programs (Chuanyi, 1989).

Variable Benefits

A long-term policy goal is to develop a system of social insurance that would be used to maintain social stability and equality by redistributing income without sacrificing economic efficiency. One suggestion toward this end is to develop a system in which benefits would vary according to urban and rural needs but would never provide less than the Five Guarantees (Chow, 1988).

In a related proposal the Ministry of Civil Affairs has also suggested that peasants in the more economically viable regions pay for their own social insurance. In less-well-developed areas the government would partially subsidize the creation of savings cooperations and welfare facilities, and areas that are classified as hardship regions would be entirely supported by the government.

Private Enterprise

There are also efforts to accommodate the needs of persons who have fallen through the safety net but who may be capable of working as private entrepreneurs. For example, in cases where older workers are not eligible for a pension, pensions cannot be awarded; or if the person is unemployed, the government allows them to obtain a licence that permits engagement in private enterprise (Tout, 1989).

Older Women

Published material available on older women and widows suggests that most elderly women depend on income and social services from the communal way of life (in rural areas) and extended family support (Barnes, 1987). Respect for elders evidently plays a major role in the well-being of older women and is an instrumental factor in strengthening their position in society. It is interesting to note, however, that government public policy discussions relating to the elderly do not refer to the special needs of older women although they often have different employment and social histories.

PRINCIPAL POLICY IDEOLOGY

The ideological approach to public services for the elderly in the PRC is dominated by the principle of social assistance whereby national, provincial, and municipal programs are typically limited to individuals who meet a needs test and have little or no recourse to family or community support. (For a detailed explanation of the development of social assistance in the PRC, see Dixon, 1981). The Five Guarantees program is illustrative of the social assistance approach, which is essentially residual in character, providing a safety net when families cannot. Program management of health and social services is a community responsibility and the national government's role is generally limited to setting standards and general goals, especially in rural areas.

Income maintenance programs function under a somewhat different ideological basis in providing benefits to populations of the industrialized urban regions. In this instance policy is moving toward the principles of social insurance in that benefits in state enterprises are earned by virtue of employment. As has been discussed, however, pension programs in the PRC lack the essential elements of social insurance as understood and practiced by industrial nations. Notably, there is no compulsory national program of pooled risks and financing that is characteristic of a social insurance system.

Limited monetary resources and practical considerations such as administrative difficulties in coping with over a billion people dispersed throughout mostly rural areas have tended to shape the strategies of social programs for the elderly. Programs have also been influenced by social, political, and demographic conditions that have helped to fashion a focus on categorically targeted groups, individual security, locally administered programs, and family and community initiatives.

ANALYSIS

It is reasonably clear that policymakers in the PRC are confronted with the difficult task of balancing social and fiscal constraints that circumscribe national intervention on the one hand and emerging forces that generate a demand for more national government involvement on the other. National interven-

tion is obstructed by an official policy of administrative decentralization, which is fortified by a widely endorsed aspiration to
rely on the resources of elderly individuals, the family, and the
community. Attempts to deal with the needs of elderly persons
on an equitable basis throughout the country, however, are
constrained by a lack of coordination among administrative units,
especially in the densely populated rural areas. National involvement is also inhibited by limited fiscal resources that can realistically be committed to the elderly population in the presence of
other demands for government support.

Inducements for more national involvement are stimulated by
an aging population and a growing incapacity of extended families
to provide adequate income and social service protection for the
elderly. Additional pressure for some form of national action
comes from the variety of income programs in state enterprises
and selected urban areas that cover only a small proportion of
workers.

Within this context, policymakers tend to define the problem
in terms that limit programs to elderly persons with measurable
needs. Consequently, the primary strategy has been to promote
social assistance programs that are designed to act as a saftey net
for demonstrably needy individuals.

This does not mean that there is an absence of interest in
expanding compulsory social insurance coverage. However,
there seems to be substantial vacillation in establishing a strategic
problem-solving approach to the expansion of old-age income
program coverage. It is apparent that a comprehensive public
pension program is not likely to be pursued in the immediate
future. This is the case, even though the shortcomings of pension
systems funded and managed by local state enterprises are
recognized as inefficient for urban employees and inapplicable
for most rural workers.

The current strategy is to experiment with a mix of quasi-social
insurance programs under the auspices of local insurance carriers
and mutual assistance funds. Concurrently, government policymakers are searching for ways to extend pension coverage to

needy agricultural workers under an assortment of diverse social assistance schemes.

The preponderance of policy activity at the national level is concerned with income maintenance provisions, such as social services and health care delivery for children and the handicapped. Thus the elderly are almost exclusively delegated to the community (Xia, 1987). This is the result of limited resources and an ideological stance relative to the government's propensity to delegate authority among administration units rather than any systematic analysis of the effectiveness of communities to respond to identified needs. There may be such studies of, for instance, the efficacy of the Five Guarantees, but they are not generally available or highly publicized.

In summary, the program strategies of care for the elderly that may be of greatest interest to policymakers in other nations is the focus in the PRC on administrative decentralization, the emphasis on social assistance programs that target the needy elderly, and the experimentations with a variety of local social insurance schemes. Each of these procedures warrants evaluation and monitoring to measure their administrative facility and effectiveness in delivering income and services to the elderly. One other important aspect of the Chinese experience that is of considerable general interest to policymakers in both industrial and developing societies, is the custom of not equating retirement from full-time employment with withdrawal from family or community commitments.

4

Kerala: Social Assistance for the Poor Elderly

Government policy goals and strategies for the elderly in India are predominantly shaped by the nation's low level of economic development (Groskind & Williamson, 1991). Policies affecting programs for the elderly on a national basis are also influenced by demographic and sociological changes manifested by increases in the number of elderly and nuclear families.

These variables have also been instrumental in old-age policy development at the state level. A distinction between national and state policies is important under India's federal system of government, which gives state legislatures the authority to develop their own programs. Thus, states may choose to participate in national income maintenance programs and, at the same time, establish their own supplementary provisions.

The southern state of Kerala has been particularly innovative in the design and implementation of old-age pension programs for its population. While it is encumbered with a poor economy, growing numbers of elderly and a rise in nuclear families, its old-age policy infrastructure is distinguished from the rest of India by two additional variables: the state's high level of education and its recent tradition of politically liberal coalition governments. These distinctive attributes account for much of Kerala's successful development of pension programs despite the adversity of having one of India's, and the world's, poorest economies.

Notwithstanding a substandard level of economic development, the state has assumed the responsibility of instituting a wide spectrum of social welfare provisions, including universal education and health care, as well as special income and service programs for children, women, and the elderly. The existence of a viable universal health care system in Kerala under untenable fiscal circumstances has been described as a paradox of economic backwardness (Chopra, 1982; Panikar & Soman, 1984). It is an equally apt description of the educational system and of state programs for the elderly, especially old-age pensions.

A sense of the level of accomplishment that the programs have attained is gained by briefly examining the number and proportion of workers who are covered by some form of retirement income in Kerala. Data on the total combined number of workers in organized and unorganized sectors covered by a retirement plan is not complete, but at least 2.6 million persons were protected by a pension, provident fund, or gratuity benefit under one of five national and state programs in 1981 (Gulati & Rajan, 1988). This approximates a minimum of 38% of the 6.8 million persons who were gainfully employed for most of the year. If all the entitlement data were collected for every public and private retirement scheme in Kerala the coverage might be as high as 50%.

A predominant reason for this level of coverage in Kerala is its highly educated population. Kerala's literacy rates of 74% for men and 64% for women is more than twice those of the national averages (Nayar, 1985). Western education, which was introduced in Kerala by missionaries in the ninteenth century, has been a particularly strong force in undermining the traditional inequitable social institutions of caste, slavery, and tenancy (Panikar & Soman, 1984). Furthermore, education has been an integral part of powerful social and religious reform movements throughout Kerala's history (Menon, 1967). It also provides the most reasonable explanation behind the lowest mortality and fertility rates in India despite lagging behind other Indian states in income, industrialization, and urbanization (Nag, 1988).

In the context of policies affecting the elderly, the high level of education has helped to structure a population that is generally more aware of conditions that have an impact on the income and service needs of workers and their dependents, including elderly persons. Both the general populace and social welfare interest groups have demonstrated an acute understanding of the needs of the elderly and of the political strategies required to establish programs that address those needs.

While education has been instrumental in empowering welfare interest groups, their influence in the policy planning process would not be possible without a receptive government. Kerala has a long history of benevolent rulers who developed a strong infrastructure of roads, schools, and hospitals (Nayar, 1983). This tradition has been continued under a series of liberal coalition governments since becoming an independent state in 1956.

The perpetuation of these traditions has, in large part, been the result of unique pluralistic governmental and social structures. A structural feature that has given the government power to implement many welfare reforms is the absence of competing power and legislative centers in village, communities and local chieftains. The composition of the densely populated state (654 persons per square kilometer) is essentially one continuous village, which leads individuals and groups to look to the state government for resources and services (Nayar, 1983). However, this has not produced a centralized, dictatorial government but, rather, has fostered a pluralistic political system made up of diverse social welfare advocates who directly participate in most stages of government decisionmaking concerning the interests of the social and economic groups they represent.

The various coalition governments since the 1950s have been especially responsive to trade unions that represent agricultural workers and to communal social welfare pressure groups composed of Hindus such as Nairs and Ezhavas, Muslims and Christians (Chander, 1981; 1986). The balance of power among these groups determines the nature of Kerala's welfare programs and their influence is felt at every step of the policymaking process, including needs assessment, goal setting, and strategic planning.

The factors that impede government action in addressing the issues of the elderly are discussed below, followed by examinations of the variables that tend to pressure the government to increase its intervention and level of current state involvement.

OBSTACLES TO FORMAL PENSION AND SERVICE SYSTEMS

Although social welfare proponents are well represented in the process of policy development, there are a number of factors that continue to thwart government, welfare advocates, and trade union efforts to respond to the needs of a growing elderly population. The most visible impediments are a low per capita income, a priority for destitute children and women, depressed levels of work activity, a high proportion of agricultural workers, an increase in the incidence of rural elderly, and a conviction that families will take care of the elderly.

Poor Economy

Poor economic conditions have played a major role in the scope and nature of the state's approach to programs for the elderly who are not protected by a pension plan. The economy in Kerala state is among the poorest in India with one of the lowest per capita income levels. A growth in economic output of 2.5% from 1980–81 to 1986–87 in Kerala is considerably below the national average of 4.5%. In the same period, the annual growth rate of per capita state domestic product in real terms was 0.6% compared to a national average of 2.3%. In 1986, Kerala's per capita income was 80% of the national average (Gulati & Rajan, 1988).

It is not surprising that Kerala also has one of the highest poverty rates in India. About 27% of the population lives below the poverty line, which is defined as the minimum income required to purchase the recommended food intake of 2,400 calories per day (Gulati & Rajan, 1988). In contrast, the national average poverty rate is 37%. The poverty rate in Kerala in rural areas is 26% and 30% in urban areas, compared to 40% and 28% in the country as a whole. Though Kerala's poverty is less compared to the national average, high literacy (and consequently high aspirations/expectations) make it more obvious than in the rest of India.

Program Focus on Youth and Women

An extreme level of poverty among children and women is the major social welfare concern of the government as expressed in the five-year plan for 1985–90 (State Planning Board, 1984). The most important welfare program in this plan is the Integrated Child Development Services. While destitute elderly persons are also targeted, the government is clearly more preoccupied with the compelling service and income needs of children and women.

Low Work Activity

Another manifestation of the poor economy is a low proportion of persons in the organized labor force, especially young people and women. A major effect that low work activity has on pensions for the elderly is that only a small proportion of the population provide a pool for contributions through payroll deductions. It also reduces the aggregate of funds available from taxes to finance noncontributory pension systems, social service, and health care programs. All of these conditions work against the viability of initiating new programs for the elderly or enhancing existing ones.

The depth of the problem of employment in Kerala is illustrated by the modest percentage of persons who worked for the major part of the year in 1981. The employment rate for men in that year was 41% and for women it was only 13%. In all of India the rates were 52% and 14%, for men and women, respectively. These rates are somewhat misleading, however, because they include children ages 0–14 which, in Kerala, make up about 35% of the population. Nevertheless, low employment is a major concern, especially with regard to young adults, as only about 22% of young men aged 15–19 and 56% aged 20–24 worked most of 1981. (In Kerala, child labor is negligible because nearly all the child population is in school.) Employment rates for women were substantially lower at 12% for ages 15–19 and 18% of ages 20–24 (Gulati & Rajan, 1988). It is important to note that in every age category, the level of participation in the labor market was significantly lower in 1981 than it had been in 1971.

The seriousness of unemployment among young people results in government policy goals that prioritize jobs for people aged 15–59. This leads to various efforts to reduce the organized work activity of older persons in the hope of opening up employment opportunities for youth, such as mandatory retirement provisions under state and national pension programs. Suggestions to raise the retirement age from 55 to 58 by some of those interested in reducing program expenditures have been met with considerable resistance from young people whose ranks have been bolstered by a recent lowering of the voting age from 21 to 18.

Agricultural Workers

The feasibility of state intervention in the care of the elderly is handicapped by the large proportion of workers and their families who live and work in agriculture. In Kerala this is not so much a problem of remote isolation, which is characteristic of many other developing societies, although some of the difficulties of administering a program to a rural population also exist in Kerala. The main difficulty is in instituting a social insurance pension system, which is based on principles of contributory funding, for people with low-wage and sporadic work patterns. Coverage of agricultural labor presents a major problem of financing benefits and services because low-income workers cannot be expected to contribute.

To some extent this is less of a problem than it was 30 years ago as the number of male cultivators and agricultural laborers has substantially declined from 48% in 1961 to 37% in 1981. For women, however, these activities account for the work of the same proportion (49%) of all female workers in both 1961 and 1981 (Gulati & Rajan, 1988).

Rural Elderly

The problem of establishing programs in rural areas is compounded by the fact that these areas have a large percentage of elderly. The elderly tend to be less educated and are often women (including many widows) who have worked in unorganized labor, thus complicating funding, qualifying, and payment mechanisms of a pension system. In Kerala 80% of the population aged 60 and over live in rural areas—78% of the state's men and 81% of the women (Gulati & Rajan, 1988).

Confidence in Family Care

The strong Hindu traditions of filial piety and kinship bonds are a part of the adherence to dharma in Kerala culture, where it is commonly assumed that the family will provide for the care of their elderly members (Nayar, 1985; Gulati & Rajan, 1988). A high level of reverence and respect for the elderly is very much ingrained in the religious and cultural practices of Kerala, as in India as a whole. The custom of caring for an elderly parent is exceptionally strong in rural areas, where the elderly have greater authority by virtue of land ownership and control over inheritance rights.

The presence of a powerful conviction in the duty of children to care for their parents serves to deflate grounds for state intervention in the form of income, social service, and health care programs. Historically, families have not only had the obligation to perform this function but also the resources to execute it. While families were not necessarily better off economically, they did not have to provide care for an extended period of time because the elderly did not tend to live long.

CATALYSTS FOR GOVERNMENT INTERVENTION

The countervailing factors that stimulate government program intervention in programs for the elderly include those that are endemic to many developing nations, such as the pressures exerted by an increase in the number of elderly persons, extended life expectancy, changes in family living arrangements, and a high percentage of widows. There are some additional factors in Kerala that are also of interest. These include the already mentioned influence of trade unions on the development of social programs and the high literacy rates of the population, as well as a decline in traditional landowner support services, and a drop in older male labor force participation.

Aging Population

All Indian states have recently shown a growth in persons aged 60 and over and a simultaneous decline in children aged 0–14, but the greatest change in both categories is in Kerala (Mammen, 1987). The growing number of elderly in the population is rapidly becoming a policy issue in Kerala. A concern for the well-being of this age group is inescapable in light of the fact that the number of persons aged 60 and over in Kerala more than doubled in the period 1961 to 1981, rising from 986,000 to 1,910,000. Moreover, this age group is projected to increase to over 8 million by the year 2026. In 1961 the proportion of persons 60 and over was 5.83% of the total population; by 1981 it had reached 7.50%; and by 2026 it will be 18.4% (Gulati & Rajan, 1988; State Planning Board, 1987). A level of 10% of the population at age 60 and over, which is sometimes used as a plateau for a society to be designated as having an elderly population, will be attained in 2001. Much of the growth in the proportion of elderly is accounted for by an escalation in the number of persons aged 75 and over, especially women.

Notably, the percentage of female elderly in Kerala has grown faster than that of the male elderly population over this period, rising at a rate of 31.2% compared to 26.5%. This contrasts with the pattern in all of India, which shows a faster rate of growth among elderly men (17.4%) than women (13.4%), although there continues to be a higher proportion of the old among women (Department of Economics and Statistics, 1986).

The changes in the elderly population negatively affect the ratio of elderly persons to persons of working age (15–59). In 1961, for example, for every 11 persons aged 60 and over there were 100 persons aged 15–59 in the population. In 1981 the ratio was 100 to 13 and in 2026 it will be 100 to 31 (Gulati & Rajan, 1988). This not only means that there are fewer people contributing taxes to pay for programs for those who do not, but also that there is a smaller proportion of caretakers who provide personal services.

Increased Life Expectancy

The rapidly growing older population is largely attributable to an increase in life expectancy. From 1941 to 1981 the life expectancy at birth rose for men from 40 to 64 years and from 42 to 68 years for women. Life expectancy at age 60 is expected to nearly triple from the years 1911–20 to 2016–20 for men from 6.9 to 20.7 years and for women from 8.4 to 22.3 years (Gulati & Rajan, 1988).

The dramatic increases in the number and proportion of longer lived persons creates severe economic hardships and psychological strain on family care givers. In the past, family stress was alleviated by a shorter period of care stemming from earlier deaths of the elderly. The increased longevity has doubled the length of care. Moreover, it is now becoming more common for the very old to be in the care of their progeny who themselves are elderly and in need of care (Nair & Tracy, 1989).

Changing Family Living Arrangements

Contributing to the problem of sustained care of the elderly are changes in traditional living patterns. As in the whole of India (Alter, 1988), Kerala is experiencing a shift from extended to nuclear families, which tends to diminish the ready availability of informal and psychological support, although children tend to continue to provide economic assistance even if there is geographic isolation from their parents. Family-based support continues as sons and daughters often assume the responsibility of caring for their parents, even when the children are poor and can ill-afford the assistance (Nair, 1990). This traditional form of support, however, may be endangered as the proportions of elderly women rise. The situation is compounded by a rising number of persons aged 70 or 80 and above, which places the burden of care on children who themselves may be 50 or 60 and above and living in poverty. There are, however, other alterations in family living arrangements in Kerala that play an important role in reducing the ability to care for elderly members.

New patterns include tendencies for women to marry at later ages, have fewer children, work outside the house, demonstrate more independence from their in-laws, aspire to different lifestyles, and have geographic mobility. While the cultural value of the role of women as caretakers for the elderly is retained, these attributes of modern society increasingly make it difficult for women to function in this capacity.

Increasing Numbers of Needy Widows

As the population ages, the proportion of women who are widowed rises. In Kerala, 63% of the women aged 65–69 are widowed and the proportion of widows aged 70 and over is 81%. In contrast, only 9% and 19%, respectively, of the men in the same age group are widowers. Widows are at particular risk as they tend to have less economic independence or recourse to retirement income than men and must rely more on the family for support. In the growing number of instances where women do not reside with immediate family members, widows become an economic and social liability (Gujral, 1987). They are also a liability to impoverished nuclear families. This problem will continually worsen in an aging population because most elderly people will be women, many of whom will be widows in need.

Trade Union Activity

As noted, an important aspect of social welfare reform in Kerala is a long-standing tradition of strong trade union activity, including the development of programs for retired workers and their dependents (Krishnamurthy, 1979). Trade unions have been instrumental in social and political changes that have helped to set the stage for a government commitment to addressing the needs of the elderly. Much of the strength of trade union coalitions of peasants' organizations and agricultural workers' unions emerged in the 1950s during the struggle to institute agrarian reforms (Menon, 1967). These and other political achievements empowered the trade unions to help establish state legislation such as the Kerala Agricultural Workers' Act of 1974, which assured a minimum wage and security of employment and introduced a provident fund scheme for agriculture workers. The influence of trade unions on pension and other social security measures has been enhanced by their participation in the decisionmaking process at all government levels (Krishnamurthy, 1979).

Diminishing Support from Landowners

Until the 1960s, a major source of support in old age was provided by the "Jajmani" system. Under this system, landlords assumed responsibility for the well-being of the older members of the family who worked for them. This system was terminated with state-legislated land and agrarian reforms in 1959 and 1965 that abolished tenancy. The reforms meant that landlords no longer assumed responsibility for medical care, shelter upkeep, and jobs suited to an elderly person's capabilities. This created a void in income and social service support for families with elderly members and consequently has helped to fuel the necessity of state intervention.

Fewer Working Elderly

An emerging issue in Kerala is the decline in the work force of men aged 60 and over, as shown by a labor force participation decrease in this age group from 60% in 1971 to 43% in 1981. In India as a whole the participation rate for men aged 60 and over in 1981 was 64%. This is of concern because it means that many of these men must now rely on sources other than employment for income, presumably the family or the state, which, in many cases, are not able to provide adequate support. The change in work patterns for men thus creates a problem for policymakers in how to fill the void.

There is less concern over the low work activity rates of older women in organized labor because patterns have not changed. The paid work activity of older women was about the same level in 1981 (7%) as it had been in 1971 (8%) (Gulati & Rajan, 1988). This does not mean that older women do not work, as most continue to perform family chores and work garden plots but, rather, their paid employment is reduced.

SPECIFICALLY DESIGNATED NEEDS

Current policies and programs indicate that the government tends to define the social and income problems of the elderly in relation to the capability of the family. The elderly population poses a problem to society only when the family cannot provide for the needs of its elderly members. There is a growing awareness that this is occurring at an unacceptable rate, particularly among lower income groups.

The government defines need within the context of the family because the family is the principal social institution for providing services and support to the elderly. This serves to concentrate government intervention to giving assistance to better enable families to fulfill their social obligations. In instances where there is no family support, the government accepts the responsibility of meeting minimum income needs.

GOALS AND STRATEGIES

At the national level social insurance functions less as a safety net than as a fringe benefit for government employees and workers in the organized sector (Groskind & Williamson, 1991). The fringe element is illustrated by the national Provident Fund Scheme for nongovernment workers, which is restricted to workers in large industries (see Chart 3). This practice reflects the national government's limited commitment to the development of pension programs that are self-funding.

This fringe benefit approach at the national level is less true in Kerala because of the presence of a well-established social welfare infrastructure (Nayar, 1985), which has given state government a clear mandate to provide pension benefits, especially for the destitute. State expenditures for pensions, for example, comprise 15% of the total state budget, virtually the same amount that is spent on health (Gulati & Rajan, 1988). In fact, expenditures on pensions as a proportion of state income have quadrupled since 1960.

By and large, the state's response to the scarcity of economic resources has been to favor income-tested programs that limit the number of beneficiaries to a manageable quantity. The basic strategy to provide old-age pensions in Kerala has been to target programs to populations that are left unprotected by national schemes. Organized workers in large industries are covered by the national employees' Provident Fund and government employees by a special system for civil servants. However, these plans exclude agricultural workers, seasonal employees, part-time, workers, and all others.

Chart 3
Provident Fund Provisions in India

Coverage. Employees of firms that have been established for at least three years and have 50 or more workers and firms using power with 20–49 workers are covered. Workers earning over Rs. 2,500 a month are excluded.

Qualifying conditions. Entitlement to the lump-sum benefit is conditional on the worker attaining age 55 and having stopped work. Payment is possible at any age if the worker has ten years of contribution, has been unemployed for six months, or is leaving the country on a permanent basis.

Benefit formula. The benefit amount is a lump-sum payment equal to the total amount of employee and employer contributions plus 11.5% interest. The fund can also be utilized before retirement for loans to cover such expenses as house construction, illness, payment of insurance policies, and buying shares of consumers cooperatives (Kareem, 1976).

Financing. The fund is financed by equal contributions of 8.33% of earnings from employees and 8.33% of payroll from employers in firms with less than 50 employees. In firms with more than 50 workers, employees pay 10% earnings and employers pay 10% of payroll plus 0.65% for the cost of administration. There is no government contribution.

Administration. The fund is administered by the Provident and Family Pension Funds under the general supervision of the Ministry of Labor.

Lacking the resources to provide coverage to all of the exempt categories of workers, the state government of Kerala has concentrated its resources on the destitute, low-income agricultural workers, and workers in selected industries that are left out of the national Provident Fund Scheme who suffer from the double burden of poverty and old age. Specifically, Kerala has implemented the Destitute Pension Scheme, the Agriculture Workers'

Pension Scheme, a variety of special funds for targeted workers, and severance pay provisions. The general attributes of each of these approaches are discussed below.

Kerala Destitute Pension Scheme

The Kerala Destitute Pension Scheme (KDP) was implemented in 1961 to help meet the income needs of three categories of the indigent. One component is the Old Age Pension (OAP), which provides benefits to elderly destitute persons aged 65 and over with limited sources of income and no relatives who can provide care. A second component is to assist physically disabled and handicapped destitute. The third component pays benefits to widowed destitute. (For a more detailed discussion of these provisions see Groskind & Williamson, 1991).

Agriculture Workers' Pension Scheme

The Agriculture Workers' Pension Scheme was implemented in 1980 to provide an old-age pension to low-income agricultural laborers (See Chart 4). The benefit is conceived as a reward for services and not as an alm or as charity (Nayar, 1985). It is financed by general revenues and is payable at age 60 to persons who have worked for at least ten years on agricultural land belonging to a landowner, whose annual income (including spouse's income and the income of unmarried sons and daughters over age 20) does not exceed Rs. 1,500 a year, and who does not receive financial assistance under other government programs. (In 1990, 1 rupee equaled about .05.) The ten-year work requirement may be waived if the applicant demonstrates physical infirmity or extreme old age. The amount of the pension is Rs. 50 a month, paid quarterly to about 280,000 beneficiaries in 1986 (Gulati & Rajan, 1988).

While women are entitled to this benefit, they account for only around 25% of the total beneficiaries (Nair, 1990). This is because of several reasons. Women are less aware of the existence

Chart 4
Agricultural Workers' Pension Scheme

Coverage. Male and female agricultural laborers who have worked for at least ten years on agricultural land belonging to a landowner. The ten-year work requirement may be waived if the applicant demonstrates physical infirmity or extreme old age.

Qualifying conditions. Benefit is payable at age 60. Annual income, including spouse's income and the income of unmarried sons and daughters over age 20, must not exceed Rs. 1,500 a year. Beneficiary must not be receiving financial assistance under any other government program. Wife is not entitled if spouse is receiving award.

Benefit formula. The amount of the pension is Rs. 50 a month, which in 1987 was about 60% of the per capita income for individuals and 47% of the per capita for households (Nair & Tracy, 1989). The benefit is paid quarterly.

Financing. The scheme is financed entirely by state general revenues.

Administration. It is administered by District Labor Offices under the auspices of the state Labor Commissioner.

---

of the pension scheme. Their applications are also prone to be more defective than men's because of higher illiteracy rates and greater difficulties in obtaining necessary documentation. Since both husband and wife are not eligible at the same time, the husband tends to apply and receive the pension and the wife forfeits her claim.

This system of an old-age pension program for destitute male and female agricultural workers is a major initiative by the state to use limited resources in extending income protection to elderly persons who live with an impoverished child and who have no access to joint or extended family support (Adiseshiah, 1981). There were nearly 278,000 beneficiaries of this program in 1985–86.

Funds for Selected Groups of Workers

A significant number of workers (about 1.25 million) are beneficiaries of state pension programs set up for special industries that are excluded from the employees' Provident Fund. These include workers who produce toddy (an alcoholic beverage made from coconuts), workers in the coir industry, fishermen, cashew workers, construction and quarry workers, coconut climbers, handloom workers, journalists, artists and writers, cinema artists, circus members, and sportsmen. The funds are financed by contributions from employees and the state. The state contributes twice the amount paid by employees (Gulati & Rajan, 1988). The coverage of the workers in these unorganized sector industries exceeds 50% of all workers in the unorganized sector.

Severance Pay

Kerala implemented the first plan in India to pay a gratuity to any worker who has completed one year of service in an industry under the Kerala Industrial Employees' Payment of Gratuity Act of 1970. Benefits are paid for superannuation or retirement as well as resignation, retrenchment, discharge, or dismissal (Kareem, 1976).

HEALTH AND SOCIAL SERVICES

There appears to be little concerted effort to design policies designated to meet the special health and social services needs of the elderly. There is some activity with regard to social services but most of it is limited to the development of geriatric nursing homes and day-care centers located in the major cities. These facilities seem to cater to the economically better off individuals who are widowed and, for a variety of reasons, prefer to live in a group setting (Gulati & Rajan, 1988; Day Care for Elderly Women, 1987).

Health Care for the Elderly

The elderly are included under the general health care provisions of the state-sponsored universal health care delivery system, which already exceeds the national targets of health status under the commitment to the goal of the Alma-Ata declaration of health for all by the year 2000 (Panikar & Soman, 1984). In many cases, however, health care for the elderly is sacrificed for younger persons. In particular, the chronically ill elderly are given tertiary care and returned to in-home care by the family because of limited supplies and hospital facilities (Gulati & Rajan, 1988). Most hospitals in Kerala are designed for short-term stays because of a lack of space. Moreover, there is no specialized training of medical care providers in geriatrics, nor special facilities. The typical pattern is for the chronically ill elderly to receive allopathic care at the state-run health center and then to return home where they rely on ayurvedic medicine (Nayar, 1985).

ANALYSIS

The conceptual framework for government policies regarding income and social service support systems for the elderly population in Kerala contrasts with the model for education and health care. Education and health care policy goals are aimed at preventing social and health problems through comprehensive, universal coverage. Unique social and political characteristics have helped to attain these goals to an extent that could not otherwise realistically be expected given the severe economic and resource limitations of the state.

There is much less political commitment and will to institute comprehensive programs to address issues concerning the elderly. The problems of the elderly are a matter of government policy concern but social welfare policy goals include the elderly as part of attempts to alleviate poverty among the general population rather than concentrating on older persons as a separate and distinct group. Prevention of poverty in old age is a component of the state's involvement in pension programs. However, there is no pretense of a preventive policy approach for the poor elderly, the government opting instead to implement curative programs to cope with the short-term needs of the elderly destitute.

Government intervention in the care of the elderly is also circumscribed because the proportion of elderly, while rising, has not yet reached a critical level. Further, the government perceives its role in addressing the needs of the elderly as supplementary to the obligation and responsibility of the family. In addition, the range of existing and potential social problems created by a budding older population is not well understood because the implications have only begun to be discussed and documented. Finally, of course, the state has very limited expendable resources for additional income support and social services for a population group whose need for government assistance is seen as less than that of children, youth, and young women.

Within this broad context, government policies for the elderly fall under two basic goals. One goal is to promote the extension of benefit coverage under national and state public old-age pension schemes. This goal seeks to improve the income level of retired workers who have earned a benefit based on their career earnings and on payroll contributions into a pension fund. This is put into effect by promoting schemes that adopt principles of social insurance, especially as they relate to financing. Accordingly, the state government is particularly supportive of pension systems for wage earners that are funded without a government subsidy. Again, relative to the pension coverage found in other societies at a similar level of economic development, a high proportion of workers in Kerala are protected by some form of retirement income.

The second goal is to provide social assistance (income-tested) benefits to categorically targeted groups of needy older persons who do not qualify for a pension. This goal is an overt acknowledgment of the difficulties of extending pension coverage to lower income workers, particularly men and women who work in agriculture. The basic short-term strategy that has been adopted is to implement programs for indigent individuals who are without recourse to family support. The elderly also benefit from other government programs that are aimed at the destitute, many of whom are older persons.

The use of a social assistance approach to income maintenance has a powerful public appeal with both practical and philosophical underpinnings. It is pragmatic because income testing controls program costs and simplifies administration, particularly funding and qualifying conditions in a society with a large percentage of workers in informal and unorganized livelihoods.

Income testing is philosophically palatable because its roots are embedded in the Gandhian concept of "Antyodaya," which is a method where the poorest of the community are given assistance first followed, progressively, by support to all those in poverty (Mohsin, 1985). This is in sharp contrast to other models of social welfare development that have been implemented in India designed to address the needs of the poor by promoting economic growth based on the theory of "percolation" or "trickle-down" welfare.

The preponderance of Kerala's government efforts in policy development for the elderly has been to provide social assistance for the destitute and gradually to extend pension programs to additional groups of wage earners. Programs for social services and health care for the elderly are discussed but are seen primarily as the function of the family with support from community organizations.

5

Mexico: Government Commitment to Social Policies for the Elderly

The role of the federal government in addressing the social, income, and health care needs of the elderly in Mexico is closely linked to a dominant national ideology that the state has the ultimate responsibility of providing social security as a basic human right for all citizens. Mexico has a tradition of a profound commitment to a universal, comprehensive system of social security that protects individuals and families from the exigencies of a money-based, industrial society: namely, loss of income due to poor health, short-term sickness, disability, old age, unemployment, and work injury. Government involvement in providing this protection is viewed as not only desirable but essential to both social justice and the development of a strong economy (Cruz, 1951). Equally important, a national system of social security is seen as critical to preserving the dignity of the individual (Aguilar, 1989).

The doctrine of social security universality is widely accepted in Latin America, including Mexico, which holds that social security is a right to all members of society as a guarantee of their social welfare (Diaz, 1979). It is a doctrine that is firmly established as an ideological goal for the governments of Latin America, reflecting endorsements of a series of labor principles and conventions that were advocated at the first Latin American social security conference held in Chile in 1942, the Declaration of Philadelphia in 1944, the Conference of Chapultepec in 1945, the Inter-American Conference on Social Security in 1947, and the 1948 Declaration of Human Rights. Even though the commitment to this doctrine has been largely symbolic in Mexico, as in many other Latin American nations, because of insufficient resources, social security as means to obtain a more humane and just society is the objective of government policy and social security is the designated technique to obtain it (Cruz, 1951; Tamburi, 1985).

BACKGROUND

A significant event in setting the role of government involvement in social programs was the Mexican revolution of 1917, which endorsed the concept that improvement of social conditions of workers strengthened their performance and, consequently, improved national economic productivity. This was an important appeal to workers because it promised a legal system to protect workers and their dependents against the risks of lost wages associated with an industrial economy.

Following the revolution, the Mexican constitution gave the federal and state governments responsibility for protecting workers and their families from the loss of income through social insurance programs. Section 123 of the 1917 constitution gives workers and families a constitutional right to social benefits and social insurance is perceived as a social benefit (Rabasa-Gamboa, 1991). It was 1925, however, before the first national social security system was established and it was restricted to federal civil servants. Coverage for the military was instituted in 1926 and for federal school teachers in 1928 (Mesa-Lago, 1978).

Program Responsibility and Authority

The local responsibility for the social welfare of other wage and salary workers was short-lived, as the constitution was amended in 1929 to centralize labor legislation, although no social security legislation was passed. The centralization of authority was a result of the accession to power of the Revolutionary National Party (PRI) in 1929 (Mesa-Lago, 1978). The new labor legislation eliminated the fragmentation of power and diverse income and health care plans that had evolved at the state level.

The 31 states in Mexico are constitutionally autonomous, but the authority of the governors, who are all members of the PRI, has been, in practice, subordinate to the president, including authority for the delivery of social welfare benefits (Aguilar, 1989). In recent years, however, there have been serious efforts to decentralize some administrative responsibilities (Inter-American Center for Social Security Studies, 1987). Although the presidential office has ultimate control, there is no single federal organization or agency that unifies supervision of the diverse social security schemes for civil servants, blue- and white-collar workers, teachers, workers in railroads, petroleum, electricity, telephone, and tobacco industries, or for a multitude of complimentary and voluntary programs (Mesa-Lago, 1978).

Despite the commitment to social security under the 1917 constitution, federal social security legislation for nongovernment employees was not passed until 1943, when nationalistic and social benevolent feelings were at a high level. The development of social security, especially health care protection, at that time was a conscious effort of the government to balance limited resources against rising need in terms of the extent of protection required to prevent unrest among the public and laborers (Aguilar, 1989). A national policy commitment to prioritize health care as the most important element of social security was an acknowledgement of the economic value of protecting workers' health in terms of productivity.

The 1943 legislation made social security coverage for income benefits and health care compulsory for the entire population under the Mexican Social Security Institute (IMSS). An innovative aspect of this doctrine was the concept of "social solidarity." Under this ideology, the IMSS was charged with providing social solidarity services to low-income and marginal groups. Importantly, social solidarity services were defined as medical care (Mallet, 1985).

Coverage of both medical care and income benefits under social insurance, however, was to be extended to population groups in stages according to social and economic conditions as determined by the executive branch of the federal government. This set the stage for a gradual introduction of social security, beginning with coverage for wage and salary workers in urban areas where systems are more readily financed and administered (Inter-American Center, 1987).

The initial effort to extend coverage to farmers and rural workers was taken in 1954 in the 13 largest agricultural areas (Inter-American Center, 1987) with additional expansion in the late 1950s and early 1960s (Mesa-Lago, 1978). In the 1970s coverage was expanded to other agricultural groups such as tobacco and sisal workers (Rabasa-Gamboa, 1991). The government revamped the civil service system in 1959 by introducing a system to consolidate coverage and expand benefits for federal employees under the Institute of Social Security and Services for Civil Servants (ISSSTE).

The experience in Mexico in the 1940s and 1950s paralleled developments in social security in Latin America as a whole. The major objectives continued to be to protect wage and salary workers against the loss of income and to provide free access to health care to workers and their dependents. The government's strategy to attain these objectives was threefold: a reliance on social insurance, investment in social insurance funds in a health infrastructure, and gradual program implementation (Castro-Gutierrez, 1988). This approach helps to explain why much of the health care is provided directly through hospitals and clinics that are owned and operated by the national government's Social Security Institute.

It is important to reiterate that government policy in Mexico has been to emphasize basic health care protection while gradually introducing income programs. Although there are provisions for income maintenance under old-age and workers' compensation laws for employees in various industries, the primary emphasis has been on the delivery of health care for the general population. Programs for the elderly as a population group that requires special attention—that is, geriatric medical care–have not been stressed outside of the public old-age pension scheme.

The ability of the nation to concentrate resources on social security, especially health care, has been simplified by the continuity of a single ruling political party, the PRI. An important impetus for continued improvement of the system is the power of pressure groups (Mesa-Lago, 1978), primarily labor unions, which make up the largest component of the PRI (IBIS Mini-Profile, 1988). Nevertheless, as noted, the planning and policymaking of the social welfare system is highly centralized with final authority in the office of the president. The authoritarian position of the government is reinforced by the presence of an informal system of bargaining and mutual accommodation used by the elite ruling class known as the "patron-peon" system (Aguilar, 1989).

Coverage under IMSS

The public old-age pension scheme of IMSS has expanded to about 42% of the economically active population (Mesa-Lago, 1986; MacKenzie, 1988) compared to 12% in 1960 and 25% in 1970 (Mesa-Lago, 1978). (See Chart 5 for brief description of the old-age pension scheme.) When the ISSSTE system for government employees is included, more than 60% are covered (IBIS Mini-Profile, 1988). While these are notable rates of coverage for employed persons, it is important to keep in mind that many people who are not designated as economically active— even though they may be looking for work, partially employed, or engaged in nonformal work—are not included in calculating coverage rates. If the total population is included, the current level of coverage amounts to only 12% of the total urban population and 3% of the rural population (Aguilar, 1989).

Chart 5
Old-Age Pension Provisions

The basic old-age pension program is under the Mexican Social Security Institute. The information that is outlined below is primarily taken from *Social Security Programs Throughout the World, 1989* (USDHHS, 1990) and Rabasa-Gamboa (1991).

Coverage. Employees in urban areas are covered, as are members of producers', agricultural, and credit union cooperatives. Voluntary coverage is possible. Coverage is being gradually extended to workers in rural areas. Public employees and petroleum workers are covered under special schemes.

Qualifying conditions. Pensions are payable at age 65 if the worker has 500 weeks of contributions. Retirement is not required if the worker secures employment with a new employer and after a six-month waiting period. Actuarially reduced benefits are payable for persons who become involuntarily unemployed at ages 60–64.

Benefit formula. The old-age pension is 35% of average earnings during the last 250 weeks of contribution, plus 1.25% of earnings per year of contribution beyond 500 weeks. If there are no dependents, the pension is increased by 15%.

Financing. The system is primarily financed by employer and employee payroll contributions. Employees contribute 1.5% of average earnings and employers contribute 4.2% of payroll for old-age pensions. The payroll tax is assessed on a maximum of up to ten times the minimum wage in the Federal District. Additional contributions are required for cash sickness and workers' compensation programs. The government contributes 0.3% of payroll for old-age pensions. For workers in cooperatives, the cooperative and the government each pay 50% of the employer-employee contributions.

Administration. The system is administered by IMSS under the general supervision of the Ministry of Labor and Social Welfare.

OBSTACLES TO GOVERNMENT INTERVENTION

Expansion of government income programs for the elderly through social insurance in Mexico has been handicapped by a variety of social and economic factors. Among the most important are these: limited national resources, problems in obtaining payroll contributions, rampant inflation and rising external debts, an incremental policy approach, family responsibility for care of the elderly, emphasis on technological and industrial development, the needs of youth and children, onerous geographic conditions, administratively independent government agencies, and political weakness of noncovered workers.

Limited Financial Resources

Limited financial resources play an important part in restricting the government role in providing pensions, health care, and social services to the elderly. The capacity of the government to respond to the needs of the aging population deteriorated following an economic crisis that began in 1981, which was compounded by serious economic repercussions caused by the 1985 earthquake (de Lehr, 1987). The unemployment, inflation, and national debt that were consequences of these events exacerbated a situation that impeded the extension of social insurance to groups that are poor actuarial risks because their benefits cannot be financed from contributions (MacKenzie, 1988).

Payroll Contributions

Difficulties in collecting payroll deductions for old-age pension coverage has been a major problem for the IMSS. Extension of coverage to farmers under legislation in the 1970s, for example, has been rescinded because the farmers have insufficient funds to make contributions.

An additional funding aspect that serves to impede business support for additional or expanded social insurance is that the proportion of employer contribution to the system is already 13.43% of payroll which is almost 75% of the total payroll tax (Rabasa-Gamboa, 1991).

Inflation and External Debt

As have other Latin American nations, Mexico has suffered from high inflation and external debt since the oil crisis of the early 1970s. This has been detrimental to the availability of resources for social programs for the general population, including the elderly. One component of these twin problems is improving, as reflected in a decline in inflation from 159.2% in 1987 to 51.7% in 1988 and 30% in 1989 (TPF&C, 1989). The external debt has substantially worsened, however, rising from 8.7% of the GNP in 1970 to 59.5% in 1987 (World Bank, 1989).

Both of these factors put pressure on the government to find mechanisms to reduce increased costs of pensions or to seek supplemental forms of insurance, such as occupational pensions and private savings. Certain aspects of this approach are frustrated, since inflation is particularly devastating to efforts to expand occupational pension schemes because employers have a problem in developing alternatives to indexing ("Benefits in Latin America Focus on Politics, Economics, Social Issues," 1987; Gerardo, 1985).

Incrementalism

The incremental approach or gradual implementation of social benefits is characteristic of centralized authoritarian governments of the region. Legislative provisions that validate this process, such as the provision in the 1943 legislation to expand coverage and benefits subject to appropriate economic and social conditions, are known as "deferment clauses." They give the executive power the authority to fix the most suitable time for applying the obligation of the legislation (Diaz, 1979) and can significantly slow the rate of federal program development. This process has been very much in evidence in the formation of social security programs.

Family Responsibility

While the government constitutionally assumes responsibility for adequate income and health care, there is a strong cultural tradition that families must also accept their obligation to care for family members. This is most evident in social services for the elderly, which receive little government attention because the family retains the primary responsibility for caring for older family members (Tapia-Videla & Parrish, 1982). This is especially true of the old in rural areas where most elderly live (Petri, 1982).

A related obstacle is evidence that old-age pensions have an impact on family size and are negatively related to birthrates in Mexico (Nugent & Gillaspy, 1983 cited in George, 1988). It is not documented if knowledge of this phenomenon has played a role in government decisions regarding the expansion of pension systems, but it is likely that such a consequence of pensions would not be well received in a society with a strong tradition of large families and reliance of the parents on the care of their children in old age.

Priority of Technology and Industrialization

Government-sponsored social programs for the elderly apparently benefited only marginally from the income that was generated by the oil industry during the economic boom of the 1970s. Most of these monies were used to expand technological and industrial development based on the theory that economic expansion would create an infrastructure that would lead to more jobs and a broader tax base to support social programs (Aguilar, 1989). The major exception has been the continued support of the health care infrastructure, which, as noted, is not specifically targeted to the elderly.

Priority of Youth and Children

Government intervention in programs for the elderly is also shaped by Mexico's large proportion of children in the population with about 43% under age 15 (Aguilar, 1989). The income, health, housing, and social service needs of this group shift policy priorities from the elderly whose perceived needs are diminished by the wide-spread belief that they are social burdens with little to contribute (Tapia-Videla & Parrish, 1982).

Geographic Impediments

The rugged terrain and isolation of many communities in Mexico create a delivery problem for federal income, health, and social service programs. Again, government programs for the elderly are greatly restricted in these areas where a substantial ratio of the population are elderly.

Administration

The government's ability to intervene is also tempered because of the administrative independence of various federal agencies, including IMSS (which enrolls 84% of all covered workers), ISSSTE (13%), public health, the armed forces, and PEMEX (the government-owned oil industry). Despite efforts since the 1960s to coordinate services among these agencies, they continue to operate under their own rules and regulations. An additional concern is that the scope of health services under the IMSS needs to be controlled or the stability of the system will be compromised.

Political Weakness

The groups of workers who have benefited from coverage of social security have been the best politically organized, typically those in urban areas. Despite gradual extension to rural unorganized workers, social security remains confined to a relatively small number of urban unionized workers (Poitras, 1973 cited in Mesa-Lago, 1978).

CATALYSTS FOR INTERVENTION

There is less published discussion of targeting programs and developing strategies to cope with the elderly in Mexico than in the other countries included in this book. Nevertheless, there are a number of elements that compel the government to give consideration to the special needs of older persons. These include the legal mandate of the constitution for social security for all, an aging population, increases in life expectancy, a growth in urban population, a rise in marginal workers, a demise in extended families, and the attraction of severance pay.

Legal Mandate

The primary impetus for expanding programs for the elderly is Article 14 of the Social Security Act of 1943, which mandates coverage of income, social services, and health care for all. While pensions have expanded to include many urban workers, in general the thrust of this mandate has been operationalized as development of health care for the entire population.

Aging Population

The proportion of elderly persons over age 65 in Mexico is relatively small at about 4.1%. This represents 3.5 million persons. The proportion of persons aged 55 and over is 8.4% or 7 million. While the numbers of elderly are beginning to be of concern, the main anxiety is for the future, when by the year 2020 it is projected that there will be 10.6 million persons aged 65 and over and 22 million aged 55 and over (Kinsella, 1988). Further, Mexico is only one of two Latin American nations (Brazil is the other) expected to have over 1 million persons aged 80 and over in 2025 (Sennott-Miller, 1989). By 2025 the ratio of persons aged 65 and over to those aged 20–64 will have risen from 8.3 to 12.9 (Torrey, Kinsella, & Taeuber, 1987). These trends threaten to destabilize susceptible service delivery systems and bring pressure to redirect traditional patterns of allocation of scarce resources (Tapia-Videla & Parrish, 1982).

Life Expectancy

Contributing to an awareness of a growing need for government intervention in providing services for older populations are increases in life expectancy. Life expectancy for Mexicans at birth rose from age 61 for women in 1965 to 72 in 1987 and from 58 to 65 for men (World Bank, 1989). Life expectancy at age 65 in Mexico in 1983 was 14.5 years for men and 15.7 years for women (World Health Organization, 1988).

Rural Population

The urban population increased from 55% of the population in 1965 to 71% in 1987 (World Bank, 1989). In many cases this has left an increasingly old and poverty-stricken rural population without protection of government programs (Tapia-Videla & Parrish, 1982).

Marginal Workers

A rise in the number of marginal workers with virtually no tax-paying capacity is creating a situation that places pressure on the governments of such countries as Mexico to develop policies that will meet the basic needs of these populations at minimum program cost. This has led to the exploration of expanding programs of social solidarity based on the principles of social assistance—income-tested benefits (Novelo, 1985).

Demise of the Extended Family

The extended family is losing its ability to care for the elderly as younger family members migrate to urban areas, as housing becomes overcrowded, and as women enter the labor market (Hoskins, 1988). Although it is estimated that only a small percentage of the elderly live alone, as early as the mid-1960s it was noted that urbanization broke down family, community, and landlord support for the elderly (Wolfe, 1968). Significant changes in the traditional extended family organization have become more of a factor in the urbanization of recent years (de Lehr, 1987).

Severance Pay

As discussed below, severance pay is a major instrument of income policy for retirees. The presence of this benefit can be detrimental to government interests in encouraging private employers to establish occupational pension schemes because of the added demand on employers (Hottinga, 1983). This serves as an impetus for policy planners to compensate for the slow development of private plans by improving the public scheme.

IDENTIFIED NEEDS

The effects of the catalysts noted above have led the government to specify in public pronouncements and legislative materials what it considers to be the major priorities of social security in general and the needs of the elderly in particular.

Primary Health Care

The government has established the delivery of primary health care as the nations' principal social program need. While the elderly population benefits from programs that improve health care services, there is little effort to address distinctive medical needs of the elderly (de Lehr, 1987).

Expanding Pension Coverage

As indicated above, while 42% of the economically active population is covered for a government pension, it is estimated that only about 12% of the nongovernment urban working population is covered. This is because unemployment is so high and a large number of workers earn a living in nonformal, uncovered work. Coverage in the rural areas outside of certain agricultural industries such as sugarcane workers is even lower. According to the National Unification Movement of Retired Persons and Pensioners (MUNJP), there are 5 million elderly with no pension coverage of any kind (Vemea, 1982). This includes women (de Lehr, 1987), farmers, and the self-employed.

Maturing Pension System

The pension system is becoming more expensive now that it is maturing and paying benefits to more retirees. This creates pressure for alternative and supplementary pension systems in preference to raising contribution rates or increasing payroll ceiling levels subject to taxes.

GOALS AND STRATEGIES

Unsatisfactory progress in expanding social security protection to rural and marginal groups in Mexican society caused the government to reorient its goals and strategies regarding social welfare and health care delivery systems in the early 1980s.

Because health care is perceived as such a critical element of social progress and justice, the focal point of change is an integration of medical care to the indigent under the IMSS system. This utilizes the resources of IMSS and its system of centralized planning combined with decentralized administration, increasing the level of community involvement and participation (Inter-American Center, 1987). The efforts to reduce federal authority and responsibility in health care delivery through decentralization in recent years is also a result of the poor economy and high inflation (Soberon, Frank & Sepulveda, 1986).

Notably, the elderly are not specifically cited in programs for improving health care to rural workers and marginal groups. Nevertheless, there are a variety of state and local social service and health care program initiatives for the elderly that demonstrate a comparable conviction in the efficacy of greater community participation in program planning and implementation.

Administration

A major concern in the delivery of social programs, especially health, has been the absence of coordination between the private, public assistance, and social security agencies, which was blamed for much of the inequitable distribution of the benefits of economic development (Soberon, Frank & Sepulveda, 1986). This issue was addressed by legislation in 1984, which set a goal of universal health coverage through the gradual implementation of decentralized authority to the states for responsibility for health care under national standards under IMSS.

COPLAMAR

A unique approach to social security for rural areas is the General Coordination Unit for the National Plan for Depressed Areas and Marginal Groups (COPLAMAR), which was initiated in 1977. This program is an attempt to link social security with economic development by stimulating the rural economy through agrarian reform, rural credit, and social insurance. The primary objective of the social insurance is to improve and expand health care coverage for the rural population of all ages (Inter-American Center, 1987). In 1983 the program was integrated with IMSS to strengthen the system through a process of decentralized administration.

Lump-Sum Payments

By law, employers must provide an old-age severance pay for unemployed persons over age 60 (Rabasa-Gamboa, 1991.) The severance pay amounts to three months' pay plus 20 days' pay per year of service (IBIS Mini-Profile, 1988). Employers are also legally bound to pay a "seniority premium" for any employment termination, including retirement, which amounts to 12 days' pay per year of covered service. When benefits from the public old-age pension scheme and private pensions are combined they equal about 70% of the average wage (Gerardo, 1985). An employee may not be dismissed because of age but if the employee refuses to retire at the age established by company policy, the right to severance pay is forfeited.

Private Plans

The government has provided effective tax incentives for the development of noncontributory private plans since 1965 (Aguilar, 1989; Munoz, 1979) as a means of supplementing the public old-age pension scheme under IMSS. Some 40% of the employers have funded pension plans (Sander & Mendoza, 1987) but the number of such plans has leveled off in recent years (IBIS Mini-Profile, 1988). Most multinational companies have savings plans, but most employee interest appears to be on short-term benefits ("Tax-Effective Benefits Take Spotlight in Brazil, Mexico, Central America," 1989).

Social Solidarity

In 1973 the government introduced a unique program of "social solidarity," which offered free medical care to low-income individuals through IMSS's health care facilities in exchange for work in public service projects. This makes it possible for persons who are not covered by social insurance to receive comparable medical care earned by public work in lieu of contributions.

Social Services

Social services, usually referred to as social benefits (*prestaciones sociales*) are beginning to expand in Latin America under national agencies because there is little tradition of established providers in the public or private sectors (Tamburi, 1985). In Mexico initial steps have been taken to increase government involvement in such measures as the establishment of the National Institute for the Elderly in 1979 ("Care of the Elderly and Rehabilitation: Mexico," 1982), the provision of 150 homes for the aged (de Lehr, 1987), and the provision of home services ("Care of the Elderly," 1987). Some geriatric centers have also been provided by the Public Assistance Department and religious institutions (Aguilar, 1989).

Other programs include a benefit for low-income elderly aged 60 and over who qualify for social services under the National System for the Integrated Family Development (DIF). Personal social services are provided, as well, to adults aged 60 and over who meet an income test. In 1984 about 12% of the 4 million elderly population received benefits from DIF (de Lehr, 1987). Services include medical care and a range of legal, food, rehabilitation, and shelter services in various geographic areas (Aguilar, 1989).

ANALYSIS

Government intervention in social welfare programs for the elderly in Mexico in this century has been fashioned by efforts to uphold an ideological constitutional and social preference, while wrestling with the reality of fiscal and administrative limitations. On the one hand, Mexican society, with government as its primary instrument, shows a strong desire to use social security as a cornerstone in building a just and economically developed nation. Universal, comprehensive social security protection against the risk of loss of income is clearly the method of choice.

Attainment of this goal has been frustrated by a lack and inefficient use of fiscal resources, administrative incapacity, and a large nonformal work sector. The most aggressive policies have focused on improving the health care delivery system, including services to the indigent, which also encompasses many elderly. Social service policies targeted for the elderly have not been a priority because they constitute a relatively small proportion of the population and extended families have been expected to meet these needs of their elderly members. Although the government continues to support the strategy of expanding income protection through the public old-age pension system, coverage remains concentrated among workers in industry in urban areas and among civil servants.

The government is under pressure to examine its involvement in meeting the income and social service needs of the elderly because of a projected growth of the elderly population in the near future (particularly the very old), an increasing rate of poor elderly in rural areas, evidence that the ability of extended families to provide care is diminishing, and its constitutional commitment.

6

Nigeria: Preservation of Traditional Support Systems

Specialists in comparative studies often question the value of studying social welfare programs for the elderly in nations, such as Nigeria, whose federal systems affect an inconsequential fraction of the population. This position has a clear bias that presumes that societies that do not rely on comprehensive federal programs are of little interest. Such a perspective overlooks the fact that neither inclusive nor centralized programs may be the long-term goal of many economically developing nations and, indeed, contrasts with efforts to retain traditional methods of support as well as with recent movements toward decentralization of government responsibility.

It is suggested here that it is precisely the limited role of the government in providing social welfare benefits for the elderly, as in Nigeria, that is of analytical interest to policymakers in many other nations. Analyzing the process of marginal government involvement increases understanding of both deliberate and unpremeditated attempts to maintain customary sources of income and social support. This is useful information to the analyst who wants to know the extent to which government strategies, including the option of noninvolvement, have had an impact on the emergence of specific models of support programs, such as industrial models of social insurance.

Government in Nigeria, as in most other African nations, has had little direct involvement in income, health, or social service programs for its older population. There is only a small percentage of workers who are entitled to retirement benefits and an even smaller proportion of elderly recipients of social services or geriatric health care (Onokerhoraye, 1984). To a large degree, this is because of greater government and social interest in addressing the education, employment, and health care needs of the young (Adeokun, 1984). But government inattention to the elderly is also the result of acquiescence to what is considered to be a traditional family and community responsibility (Jack, Adeokun, & Jaiyesimi, 1984). Moreover, there is little reason for the government to intervene as family networks continue to be the mainstay of support for elderly persons in both urban and rural areas (Adeokun, 1984; Ekpenyong, Oyeneye, & Peil, 1986).

Nigeria, then, is of analytical interest because government policy has assumed a detached posture to the needs of most elderly, especially nonwage earners who comprise most of the work force. It is also of interest because, as the continent's most populous nation, roughly estimated to be 107 million people in 1987 (World Bank, 1989), Nigeria plays an important economic and political role in African affairs. The government's level of involvement in social welfare for the elderly is followed with some interest among other former British colonies that share a legacy with respect to certain government income maintenance programs, especially provident fund systems. This includes The Gambia, Ghana, Kenya, Swaziland, Tanzania, Uganda, and Zambia, which frequently join Nigeria in participation at regional seminars and training conferences on social security issues sponsored by the International Social Security Association (ISSA).[1]

GOVERNMENT INTERVENTION IN SOCIAL WELFARE

The level of government intervention in the delivery of social welfare policies and programs in Nigeria is constrained by a federal administrative structure and a host of discordant political factions (Tartter, 1982). Although there is a strong central government, what the government can do, if it chooses to do it, is tempered by the structure of a federal system that delegates specific authority to the 19 states and over 300 local governments representing the diverse political wills of hundreds of ethnic groups.

Government involvement is also shaped by a commitment to an ideological blend of socialist and capitalist strategy in both its economic and social welfare delivery systems (Sanda, 1987). In terms of government organization, the goal of this mixed approach is to achieve an equilibrium between federal government obligations and local and individual responsibilities. With regard to the elderly, deferring responsibility for support to families and communities is combined with a pledge of government solidarity that assures all elderly citizens of suitable and adequate old age care and pensions under the constitution. This promise, however, must be viewed with considerable caution as the extent to which constitutional obligations are simply rhetoric is unclear, especially when they require federal resources.

The establishment of a national provident fund scheme (discussed later) contributed to the legitimacy of the government's resolve to portray itself as a federal system. Its implementation was part of the concept of a "federal character," which has been a major strategy since independence to promote the integration of the various ethnic groups (Kirk-Greene, 1986) because it gave them a vested interest in government-sponsored programs (Williamson & Pampel, 1988). Efforts to stabilize cohesiveness among the diverse ethnic groups and regions through an established federal role in policy development and program administration continues to be an important rationale for government intervention in income and health care systems, although this is aimed more at the general population than at the elderly.

The government appears to be interested in proceeding with involvement in income support programs for the elderly through the provident fund system, but there is little effort beyond that. Even if the government had wanted to pursue additional intervention in program development for the elderly, it would have been impeded by the economic trends of recent years. Nigeria experienced the extremes of a boom economy in the 1970s and a recession in the 1980s that reflected dramatic fluctuations in the world oil market. The instability that continues to reverberate from vacillating oil prices would substantially affect any government attempts to be involved in assuming greater obligations to financially support income, health, and social services programs for the elderly.

The political precariousness of Nigeria since independence is apparently not a major factor in the level of public social welfare programs. Although political rule alternated between democratically elected leaders in 1960–66 and 1979–83 and military leaders in 1966–79 and 1983 to the present (Williamson & Pampel, 1988), civil law has been maintained by the steady control of the civil service and military.

National Provident Fund

The principal system of retirement income is the National Provident Fund (NPF) scheme, initiated in 1961, which is limited to workers, virtually all male, in industries of ten employees or more. (See Chart 6 for major program features.) The program is intended to provide a minimum level of benefits for workers who retire, die, or become sick or unemployed. It is a contributory system based on payroll tax deductions from employers and employees that awards accumulated contributions plus interest in a lump-sum payment at retirement at age 55.[2]

There are over 2.5 million workers covered under the scheme, which is roughly 7–9% of the economically active population between ages 15 and 54 (based on 1983 data from the International Labour Office's *Yearbook of Labour Statistics 1987*). This underestimates total coverage of wage and salary earners, however, because it excludes a sizable federal and state civil service that is covered under a government pension fund, and state government parastatals. Data on the total number of workers

Chart 6
National Provident Fund of Nigeria

Information on the provisions under the National Provident Fund is primarily based on *Social Security Programs Throughout the World, 1989* (USDHHS, 1990) and supplementary information from Sanda (1987) and Ogunshola (1979).

Basic Law. The National Provident Fund Act was established in 1961 following independence from Britain.

Coverage. Employed persons in business and firms with 10 or more employees. Federal and state civil servants and universities are covered under a separate scheme.

Qualifying conditions. Anyone who has been employed in covered work qualifies for a retirement benefit when they reach age 55. Payment will not be made if the worker continues to be engaged in regular employment. The benefit is payable at any age if the worker is permanently disabled, emigrates permanently, or dies.

A worker who has been unemployed for at least one year may withdraw up to one-half of the total contribution paid in, exclusive of interest. This may be done at any age.

Benefit formula. The benefit is a lump-sum payment equal to the sum total of contributions made by employee and employer plus interest at 4% per annum compound.

Financing. The system is fully funded by payroll contributions of 6% each from employees and employers. The funds from these contributions also finance cash sickness benefits and are used as investment capital by the state. The government does not provide any subsidy.

Administration. Since 1975, the National Provident Fund has been administered by a semiautonomous board consisting of representatives from employers' associations, trade unions, the Central Bank, and the Ministries of Finance, Establishments, and Economic Development. The board is chaired by the permanent secretary of the Federal Ministry of Labour. General supervision of the fund is under the Ministry of Employment, Labour, and Productivity.

enrolled in civil service pensions are not available, but in 1979 it was estimated at less than 3 million (Ogunshola, 1979). Assuming that this figure has not declined, when combined with the current approximately 2 million workers in the NPF, a very crude estimate of the total proportion of economically active population between ages 15 and 64 who are covered for either a public provident fund or pension is 20%. This proportion does not include an undetermined number of workers covered under private occupational pension schemes that operate in the larger industries in Nigeria (Bell, 1985). Apparently, few women are covered by either the public provident or pension schemes.

The NPF has continued to develop over the years, primarily because it is an effective means of accumulating capital for financing investments through enforced savings of employer and employee contributions. Its longevity is also a result of tenacious support among the numerically large and politically powerful civil service, which is responsible for the management of the fund. The system was, in fact, created largely because of the efforts of professionals in the civil service who were aware of the implementation of similar schemes in other former British colonies and of the introduction of social insurance programs in other newly independent African nations (Williamson & Pampel, 1988). Under military rule the traditional role of the civil servants has been converted from advisers and administrators into policy-makers and rulers as part of the executive branch of government (Oyovbaire, 1984).

It is important to note that both provident fund and social insurance schemes were relatively easy to introduce in the newly independent African nations such as Nigeria because their small proportions of older persons required a minimal financial commitment (Mouton, 1975). In addition, qualifying conditions based on contributions and years of service meant that it would be several years before benefits had to be paid out and, in the meantime, the government could use the accumulated trust funds for economic development and investments. In recent years, the fiscal problems that confront some African social insurance schemes are due to maturation, which means that there are more recipients of benefits, creating a strain on the fund's fiscal balance. In Nigeria, for example, the total benefits awarded under the NPF in 1983 were about 7,689,000 naira (about U.S. $9.7 million in 1985 exchange rates) compared to only 40,000 naira ($50,400) paid in 1963 (Federal Ministry of Employment Labour and Productivity, 1985).[3]

Public Service Pensions

Federal and state government workers are entitled to both a gratuity payment and a pension if they have completed at least 15 years of covered employment. Retirement is compulsory after an unknown (possibly 30) specified number of years of service, which means that many retire in their 50s and 60s (Peil et al., 1985), thus enabling younger workers to fill their positions. The maximum benefit is for 35 years of service when the gratuity amounts to 300% of the final salary and the pension is equal to 70%. Normal retirement age is 60 but there are generous early retirement provisions and an unreduced pension can be taken as early as age 45 (Ogunshola, 1979; Bell, 1985). In addition, there are numerous state government pension programs, referred to as parastatals, which are financed like the NPF but award benefits similar to the federal public civil service scheme (Bell, 1985).

OBSTACLES TO GOVERNMENT INTERVENTION

There are numerous and significant impediments to expanding the role of government in providing income, health, and social service programs for the elderly in Nigeria. As indicated above, the most powerful constraints are cultural and historic preferences among the government and public alike for a continuation of nongovernment support systems of extended families and communities. Any prospects of increased government involvement are rendered even more unlikely by an absence of public trust in government, inadequate administrative facilities, a predominately rural population, and a growing proportion of informal workers in urban areas as discussed below.

Extended Family

As in most other African nations, the elderly in Nigeria are viewed from an enduring tradition of pride and importance both in the family and in the community (Rwezaura, 1989). The introduction of Christianity, public education, a money economy, and urbanization under colonial rule, accentuated, at least ideologically, the rights of individuals over kinship and community (Ekpe, 1983; Rwezaura, 1989), and these are often blamed for contributing to a gradual disintegration of extended families. Despite this contention, research suggests that extended families have not been destroyed by modernization/urbanization and continue to provide for their elderly members in both urban and rural areas (Onokerhoraye, 1984; Ekpenyong, Oyeneye, & Peil, 1986; Peil, 1991).

The reverence that is still accorded old persons is augmented by the continued participation of elders in family and village meetings, in helping to raise their grandchildren, and in passing on oral history and customs (ISSA Document, 1981; Ekpenyong, Oyeneye, & Peil, 1986). In turn, most elderly still receive support from the immediate family, the extended family, and community (Ijere, 1966; Ekpe, 1983; Adeokun, 1984; Sanda, 1987; Tout, 1989; Peil, Bamisaiye, & Ekpenyong, 1989; Peil, 1991).

The extent to which children provide income support for their parents is documented in a recent study of Southern Nigeria, which found that less than 3% of urban elderly and 7% of village elderly received no financial or material support from family or relatives (Ekpenyong, Oyeneye, & Peil, 1986). Such customs effectively reduce rationales for government intervention (Adeokun, 1985 cited in Habte-Gabr, Blum, & Smith, 1987).

There is also less need for government intercession in a society, such as Nigeria, where there are few elderly members of the extended family who are totally functionally incapacitated and require full-time care (Adeokun, 1984). It is still unusual for the elderly to live beyond age 75, when the incidence of incapacity is likely to occur.

Public Confidence

There is a lack of public confidence that is required to generate support for government program involvement. The state's ability to govern fairly has been subject to question given widespread corruption (Kirk-Greene, 1986). An ethnically divisive population is yet another source of public distrust of federal programs with centralized authority. A suspicion of the motivation of both government and private enterprises in providing pensions helps to explain an absence of public demands for retirement programs by trade unions.

Inadequate Administration Capabilities

A major deterrent to increasing government intervention is an inadequate social welfare infrastructure, a shortage of experienced administrative personnel, widespread illiteracy, and communication difficulties (Mouton & Gruat, 1988). Even the lack of such routine operations as mail delivery can be an insurmountable obstacle to an effective and reliable service system. One researcher suggests that these factors are more important in the reluctance or inability of governments to intervene than the belief that the community should be responsible for providing care for the elderly (Ijere, 1978).

Rural Population

Another disincentive for the government to become more involved in program development is the large proportion of the general population who live in rural areas. In 1987 the percentage was estimated at 67%, reflecting a decline from 83% in 1965 (World Bank, 1989). In a geographically spacious country such as Nigeria (with 357,000 square miles [924,630 square kilometers], which is larger than California, Oregon, and Washington combined) it is extremely difficult to administer federal income or social service programs to isolated villages.

Informal Nonwage Earners

A growing problem that impedes government intervention is that of extending programs to persons who are in the informal work sector. These workers earn their living by selling goods and services in the street economy or in jobs where payment records are not maintained. The attraction of nonformal labor is that workers may earn more by working for themselves than for wages. They can also use their earnings for reinvestment and daily living.

The problem also extends to low-income earners in the formal work sector, as it is particularly problematic for the government to expand any form of social insurance or enforced savings program to populations that have a very low per capita income and a high proportion of in-kind remuneration for work (Williamson & Pampel, 1988).

Absence of Interest Group Support

Government involvement in income programs for the elderly has not been a priority issue with political parties or with trade unions either before or after independence (Williamson & Pampel, 1988). In part, the lack of concern among the unions for improved income systems at retirement is a result of the division within the ranks of labor, but it may also be attributable to a general distrust of the motivation of both the federal government and employers in private industry. On at least one occasion, the implementation of a pension scheme in a major multinational company was successfully resisted by labor on the grounds that the pension benefits would be used to exert pressure against further unionization (Sadri, 1987). Moreover, workers want more flexibility to move in and out of wage employment.

National External Debt

The fiscal ability of the government to extend income protection under the NPF, to develop more social services for the elderly, or to introduce geriatric medical care is greatly limited by the presence of an enormous national external debt. The magnitude of this debt is attested to by a growth from only 4.3% of the GNP in 1970 to 111.3% in 1987 (World Bank, 1989).

CATALYSTS FOR INTERVENTION

Despite the presence of the factors noted above that make further government involvement implausible, there are equivocal pressures for the government to assume a greater capacity in addressing the needs of older persons. Much of this simply has to do with the demographic changes reflected in a growing number of old and very old persons who strain the capacity of traditional sources of support.

Nigeria is a country dominated by youth with over one-third of its population aged 9 or younger in 1983 (International Labour Office, 1988), but the ratio of older persons is sufficient to warrant concern. As of 1986, the population aged 50 and over was estimated to be 9% (8.5% men and 9.4% women), 6.3% were 55 plus and 2.5% were 65 and over (United Nations, 1986b). Of importance to policymakers is the long-range projected growth rate, which indicates that the number of persons in the 60 and over age group will escalate by 169% from 1970 to 2020 (ISSA Document, 1981). Also of significance is the projection that there will be 1.2 million Nigerians aged 80 and over by 2025 (American Association for International Aging [AAIA], 1985). An indicator of future growth in the proportion of older people is the increase in the average life expectancy at birth, which rose for men from age 40 in 1965 to age 49 in 1987 and from age 43 to 53 for women over the same period (World Bank, 1989).

As noted, traditional family support systems are firmly in place, yet there are signs that in certain circumstances, there is less care available to the elderly than in the past. This assumption, however, tends to be based on anecdotes, subjective observations, and biased surveys, rather than empirical data. More scientifically derived information is difficult to obtain because there are no previous studies conducted on the level of care by which to compare. In fact, research indicates that older people tend to romanticize about the status of the elderly in the past and the level of family and community support (Ekpenyong, Oyeneye, & Peil, 1986; Peil, Bamisaiye, & Ekpenyong, 1989).

The government has gradually assumed much of the political and social power from the elderly who have gradually lost control over the allocation of land resources and over civic authority (Adeokun, 1984; Jack, Adeokun, & Jaiyesimi, 1984). Land is now gained through personal achievement and paid employment rather than age and inheritance. Civic authority has been wrested from elderly rulers through a political system that has replaced the native administrative system.

International Pressure

As a participating member of international and African organizations, Nigeria has an official obligation to adhere to International Labour Office, World Health Organization, and African conference conventions and standards regarding minimum benefits and services to the elderly. This is not an inconsequential consideration, because participation as an equal among both African and other nations is of considerable importance to Nigeria's prestige (Babangida, 1987). Nevertheless, it is difficult to ascertain exactly how these obligations are translated into program reality. A certain willingness to work toward conforming to these standards, however, is reflected in Nigeria's participation in international and regional conferences on aging, such as the 1982 World Assembly on Aging for which Nigeria was cited as representative of countries keenly aware of the problem of aging in the context of high fertility (AAIA, 1985). Preconference preparation included special studies and committee reports that accentuated the awareness of current and potential problems of the elderly in Nigeria.

Urbanization

First stimulated by the oil boom in the 1970s, urban drift grew at an alarming rate (Kirk-Greene, 1986). As adult children migrate to urban areas their parents typically stay at their rural homes. While the adult children generally send money home, they cannot provide personal care, help perform household chores, or easily convey emotional support (ISSA Document, 1981; Adeokun, 1984; Jack, Adeokun, & Jaiyesimi, 1984). A growing concern is for the loss of daughters who are the traditional providers of care to elderly parents. Many young women who become educated move to urban areas to pursue interests that keep them physically separated from their parents (Ekpe, 1983). Yet research shows that even in urban areas older women are part of a three-generation household (Peil, 1991).

Industrialization

Industrialization and mass production have had an adverse consequence on the ability of many elderly persons to remain in, or to secure, economically rewarding employment either on a full- or part-time basis. The individuals who are most affected are local craft workers and persons engaged in cottage industries who cannot compete with products that are produced more inexpensively by cheap labor in the large manufacturing industries of the cities. Small-scale enterprises continue to be an important source of earnings but some older persons are adversely affected by a lack of raw materials and increased mass production of quality goods at cheaper prices that, in many cases, are produced by the sons and daughters who have left the rural areas to work in industry.

SPECIFIC IDENTIFIED NEEDS

As noted, an indication of the government's interest in the elderly is a succession of conferences, meetings, and government documents. While such reports do not affirm that they have actually resulted in any action, a useful indicator of government goals and objectives is to examine how it perceives the issues involved with an aging population and potential ways of addressing them.

Recognition of Need

As early as the beginning of the 1970s, the Nigerian government was investigating the social welfare needs of the elderly. In 1974 a conference of government officials recommended a national seminar on the topic and commissioned a national research project that was undertaken in 1980 (ISSA Document, 1981). A follow-up workshop on aging was held in Lagos in 1981, which brought together experts from various African nations to prepare a report to be used as the basic document for the African region's participation in the 1982 World Assembly on Aging in Vienna. The report was also to be used in the planning of policies and services in Nigeria.

The overriding theme of these and other government documents is to do nothing that might jeopardize the role of traditional family support. Whether this is a convenient rationale to continue a laissez-faire approach or a genuine belief that government involvement on the scale of programs in industrial societies will weaken family support systems is not known. Regardless, the various statements of available documents indicate that the residents of the small towns and villages are expected to abide by tradition and provide for their elderly.

Identified Needs

The specific needs of the elderly that were identified by the government in preparing the World Assembly report and that continue to be of primary concern are dependency, labor force participation, old-age income security, and health, education, and social service provisions (ISSA Document, 1981).

Special Needs of Women

It has been nongovernment research that has inventoried the special needs of elderly women. Studies show that they tend to receive less support in their own homes than older men who have wives to care for them. Elderly women often return to their natal homes or join the household of a married child to help care for the grandchildren. These women, however, are not likely to have the same level of domestic assistance as older men and, yet, are often subject to strenuous physical labor (Peil, Bamisaiye, & Ekpenyong, 1989). Moreover, women over age 85 are more liable to live alone.

GOALS AND STRATEGIES

Government goals and strategies are unquestionably tempered by a lack of fiscal resources, but they are also strongly influenced by the belief that any solutions to the problems of the elderly population must be approached in the context of Nigerian, not European or North American, cultures (Oriol, 1982; Ekpe, 1983; Jack, Adeokun, & Jaiyesimi, 1984). As noted, this is interpreted as programs and policies that will foster family and community-based services (Nigeria, 1983) and preserve the traditional role of the elderly in family and community decisions (AAIA, 1985).

Conversion of Provident Fund to Social Insurance

Ever since its inception in 1961, the National Provident Fund has been targeted for eventual conversion to a social insurance system. This has been a central policy issue in former British colonies for many years, although few have actually made the conversion. In Nigeria attempts to change to a comprehensive social insurance scheme are justified in that such a scheme would utilize the available bank of trained manpower, decentralize program operations to the district level, and institute benefits that will provide lasting income after retirement (Kisilu, 1986; Dixon, 1987).

A variety of interest groups, including trade unions, have been opposed to dropping the NPF in favor of social insurance (ILO, 1977, cited in Williamson & Pampel, 1988). Although the functions of the civil service have remained relatively stable despite sudden changes of government, there is doubt that the government can always guarantee payment of a pension to which individual workers contribute over a lifetime. There simply is no dependable mechanism that would guarantee that the government in power at the time a worker retires in the future would make good on a prior regime's promise to pay benefits in installments from the worker's retirement until death. Also important is the absence of any mechanism to control benefit levels for inflation.

Federal, State, and Local Governments

As noted, the constitution and the five-year development plans target the elderly for social welfare policies and programs at the federal and state levels. In practice, this goal may have little meaning because of other priorities, limited resources, and a preference for utilizing traditional values and institutions to achieve national objectives in caring for the elderly (Jack, Adeokun, & Jaiyesimi, 1984).

Health Care for the Elderly

A problem for modernizing health care delivery in compliance with meeting the needs of the elderly under the World Health Organization's health care for all by the year 2000 campaign is the conflict with the traditional values and preferences held by many older persons, especially their beliefs in magical and supernatural causes and treatments of ill health (Adeokun, 1984). In theory, the government acknowledges the value of providing for geriatric health care training of medical personnel, fostering employment of elderly, and establishing community centers and clubs. In actuality, however, these efforts have been only marginally instituted. There is a particularly acute absence of geriatric care for elderly persons in rural areas (Ebomoyi, 1989, cited in *Ageing International*, 1989)

Participation

A controversial strategy involves what the government claims is an effort to improve traditional family and community support systems by increasing the level of participation of the elderly in the decisionmaking process regarding policies and programs that will affect them (ISSA Document, 1981; AAIA, 1985). The dispute is whether this would actually raise their influence or if it is a tactic that is really aimed at weakening the power they already have. The plan is to establish state and local councils made up of elderly community members. The councils would serve not only to administer local programs but to gather heretofore unavailable basic data on the needs of the elderly in a given area. An essential facet of the data gathering would be public input in order to help make the councils effective interest groups.

Under the plan, the councils would also provide improved coordination among state and federal government services. This approach is supposedly devised both to reduce the need for federal expenditures of limited resources and to reinforce strongly held convictions about relationships between children and their parents and about the venerated status of the elderly. There is no available research or information to verify, or refute, the purpose or wisdom of the plan.

Voluntary Organizations

A tactic of government policy to help keep it free of responsibility for elderly support and services is to encourage community volunteers to provide the elderly with home-based care. Self-help groups have also been suggested. These efforts have had little impact, however, because they have not been provided with any resources (Adeokun, 1984), which would, of course, require at least a modicum of government resources.

Employment for the Elderly

As in some other African nations (UNCSDHA, 1981), the Nigerian government has expressed an interest in enhancing the work contribution of older persons, which also tends to strengthen family ties. This was supposed to have been brought about by reducing arduous labor conditions for farmers, reactivating small-scale village industry that utilizes the skills of older persons, and protecting the jobs of older workers (ISSA Document, 1981). Apparently, however, no action has been taken to make this a reality. In fact, one recent study indicates that elderly persons are compelled by economic considerations and by government to migrate to rural areas so that they may engage in subsistence farming (Ebomoyi, 1989, cited in *Ageing International*, 1989). In practice, most elderly persons continue to work into their 60s and many into their 70s and 80s (Peil, Ekpenyong, & Oyeneye, 1985). Women tend to leave the work force at somewhat earlier ages but continue to have alternate roles as grandmothers and homemakers (Ekpenyong, Oyeneye, & Peil, 1986).

Occupational Pensions

Another attempt at limiting the need for government involvement is the promotion of occupational (private) pension schemes. At the same time in 1961 that the NPF was established, legislation was passed to stimulate the development of occupational pension plans through tax incentives. The government benefited from this arrangement by requiring a set percentage of the accumulated private pension funds to be invested in government bonds (Ogunshola, 1979; Bell, 1985). Unfortunately, there are no data available to determine how successful this strategy has been.

ANALYSIS

Nigeria is representative of other African nations that are responding to an increased awareness of the social and income problems of their elderly populations by assessing the role of government in addressing these problems. For the most part, the government role has been one of noninvolvement, leaving the responsibility for care of the elderly to individuals and families. Persuasion for increased involvement comes primarily from international organizations to expand old-age income protection to more workers and to convert the provident fund into a social insurance scheme. This has been stymied by limited fiscal resources, political instability, external debts, an undeveloped social welfare infrastructure, an uninsurable informal work sector, ethnic divisiveness, and opposition of trade unions and other interest groups.

An increasingly important factor in keeping the level of government intervention at a minimum in policies for the elderly is the conviction that solutions must be conceptualized from the Nigerian historic experience of traditional support systems. This is not a rejection of the industrial model of social security protection; rather it is an attempt to modify its necessity through preventive measures. The industrial model of support for the elderly is coming to be viewed as a stopgap or safety-net measure that requires restraint to prevent its benefits from weakening the motivation for family and community care of older persons. It is often perceived, rightly or wrongly, that the industrial model of social security has contributed to the demise of family support and networks in economically developed nations and a major social and government objective of Nigeria is to avoid this from happening in its society.

It is assumed that a shoring up of the traditional means of support would not encompass some of the elements of prior customs, such as the economic subordination of women and young men that assured their dependence on male elders (Rwezaura, 1989). Rather, a government goal of using policies and programs to strengthen customary methods of support involves steps to improve equity among the generations through participation in the decisionmaking process. A tactical approach under consideration is to assist communities and regions in establishing local organizations that will allow for increased representation of the views and of the elderly themselves with regard to their needs and ways of addressing them. Significantly, locally based organizations would also permit an improved method of data gathering and administration of programs oriented to local needs.

There is great interest in other African nations with a growing number of at-risk elderly in policies and programs that will strengthen the role of the family and community (African Conference on Gerontology, 1984; Omari, 1987; Zimbabwe Action Plan on the Elderly, 1986; Woodman, 1986). Whether the government will intervene to bolster traditional support systems for the elderly in Nigeria remains to be seen.

NOTES

1. For more detailed information on social insurance programs in English-speaking African nations, including summaries of regional conferences, see issues of *African News Sheet* published by the African Regional Office of

the International Social Security Association in Lome, Togo, and issues of the *International Social Security Review*.

2. There is disagreement over the official retirement age under the NPF. According to the International Social Security Association (1989) and the U.S. Social Security Administration's Office of International Policy it is age 55 (see *Social Security Programs Throughout the World-1989*, 1990), but Peil (1991) maintains that it is age 60.

3. One Nigerian naira was equivalent to about 1.26 U.S. dollars in 1985.

7

Turkey: Phased Development of Policies and Programs for the Elderly

The old-age pension system in Turkey is noteworthy because of its advanced level of development in spite of a youth-dominated society and limited financial resources available for programs for the elderly. The proportion of workers and their dependents and survivors who are covered by social insurance is relatively high and there are beginnings of successful expansion to rural areas. Health care provisions for pensioners and their dependents are also fairly well established, although public social services for older persons are only just commencing.

Income maintenance and health care programs for the elderly owe much of their success to a 1961 constitutional proviso (Article 60) and subsequent amendments that require the state to assure all of its citizens protection from the risk of the loss of income due to disability, old age, and death. Everyone has a right to social security and the state assumes the obligation of ensuring that right (Danisoglu, 1987). The law, however, allows for the mandate of state intervention to be fulfilled on an incremental basis over an unspecified period of time.

Moreover, current policy does not advocate a rush to create comprehensive, centrally managed government programs for the elderly. Although the state accepts the obligation to develop policies and programs that will assist the elderly, it promotes the family as the basic unit of care. In this context, the government has deemphasized social services that can be rendered by family caretakers in favor of programs that replace a portion of lost income for designated workers. The goal of extending coverage to all is being attained by gradually expanding social insurance coverage to previously excluded groups of workers and their dependents.

The phasing in of programs is augmented by government policy that is strongly biased toward the model of compulsory, contributory social insurance. The state is averse to any system that requires government expenditures, so it is particularly important that programs have the capability of funding themselves. This policy serves to restrict insurance coverage to groups of workers whose source of income is suitable to employee and employer contributions based on payroll deductions. It is a policy that makes it difficult to include agriculture workers, especially seasonal workers and self-employed farmers.

It is also a policy that functions within economic realities. Turkey's per capita GNP of $1,540 in 1981 is by far the lowest in Europe and on a par with that of Costa Rica, Jordan, Paraguay, and Syria (World Bank, 1984). Similar to the situation in many developing nations, Turkey has a substantial national external debt, which rose from 33.5% of GNP in 1980 to 49.2% in 1985 (World Bank, 1987). When viewed from a short-range policy perspective of cost-effectiveness, it is difficult to justify spending limited general revenues on a small segment of the population when there is the alternative of funding a social insurance program through payroll contributions. While this limits coverage, it curtails government expenditures.

Another aspect of pension policy in Turkey that merits attention goes beyond a constitutional requirement for protecting workers and their dependents. Increasingly, government policy reflects an acceptance of the concept that social welfare programs, including insurance programs targeted for the elderly, are a critical component of the nation's economic development. This has resulted in the integration of social insurance as a major element in economic planning, as well as in planning for social development (Social Insurance Institution, 1986). As such, income maintenance programs have become a regular feature of the government's five-year development plans.

Coverage

The proportion of workers and dependents covered by one of three state-managed social insurance schemes is quite high given the level of Turkey's economic development. Coverage in 1989, as a percent of the working population, was estimated to be 45.4%. In 1985 it was 40.4% and it was only 28.5% in 1978 (OECD, 1985). The increase since 1978 is nearly 60%.

The number of workers covered has steadily risen from 3.5 million in 1974 (Roberts, 1976) to 4.6 million in 1980 (Madazli, 1983), reaching 6.3 million in 1987 (Bag-Kur Insurance Institute, 1987). This represents an increase of 80% over the period 1974 to 1987 and 37% since 1980. In addition, there continues to be a number of persons working in Europe who are covered under social insurance by virtue of bilateral agreements with Turkey, although the number working abroad has declined sharply in recent years.

Basic Social Insurance Systems

There are three state social insurance systems that operate separate invalidity, death, old-age pension, and social assistance programs. These are the Social Insurance Institute (SII), the Bag-Kur Insurance Institute, and the Civil Service Fund. The largest of these institutions, established in 1965, is SII, which provides coverage for wage earners. In 1987 it had about 2.9 million insured members (Bag-Kur Insurance Institute, 1987). There are nearly 10 million persons receiving benefits of whom 9 million are dependents. The contingencies protected by SII are in basic accordance with the minimum standards of ILO Convention 102 regarding medical care, sickness, and old age. SII provides benefits in the event of all risks associated with wage loss with the exception of unemployment and family allowances (SII, 1986) (see Chart 7).

Chart 7
Basic Old-Age Pension Provisions In Turkey

Each of the three basic social insurance systems provides protection against the loss of income for retirement, invalidity, and death. Benefits are payable to survivors and dependents. Income-tested benefits are also payable to workers who have not been employed long enough to qualify for full benefits.

Coverage. Employees in industry and commerce are covered under the Social Insurance Act. This program was first established in 1949. Self-employed small businessmen, craftsmen, and certain tradesmen have been covered under a special scheme (Bag-Kur) since 1972. Since 1984 self-employed farmers who are heads of households are covered. Civil servants belong to a special fund first instituted in 1950.

Qualifying Conditions

Social Insurance Institute. Workers under SII must work in covered employment for 20 years and have reached age 55 (men) and 50 (women). As of 1990 the age of first entitlement will become 60 and 55 for men and women, respectively. Retirement is required for benefit payment.

Bag-Kur. Under the Bag-Kur system, a beneficiary must have reached age 55 (men) and 50 (women) and contributed for 25 years. Retirement is required until the recipient reaches age 60.

Civil Service Fund. Civil servants are eligible for a pension at any age after the completion of 25 years of service. A person may receive a benefit at age 60 with at least ten years of covered employment.

Benefit Formula

Social Insurance Institute. The basic benefit amount for a person under SII is 60% of average earnings over the last five years. Recorded earnings for prior years are adjusted by statutory coefficients. A reduced pension is payable to persons with less than 20 years of coverage. The pension is reduced by 1% for each year of insurance under 20 years. There is a minimum and a maximum benefit and benefit amounts are indexed for adjustment to inflation every two years.

Bag-Kur. The pension amount is based on a monthly income class or grade of the insured person at the rate of 70% of the result of multiplying the index figure by 30. The rate is increased by one percentage point for each contribution year in excess of 25 years and by another one percentage point for each year above aged 55 (men) and 50 (women). A partial pension is payable to persons ages 55 (men) and 50 (women) with at least 15 but less than 25 years of coverage. Each pensioner receives a supplementary allowance.

Civil Service Fund. The pension is 70% of the result obtained by multiplying a factor related to the factor used to calculate the recent monthly salary of the beneficiary and a coefficient established each year in the national budget. Each pensioner receives a supplementary allowance. There is a minimum benefit.

Financing

Social Insurance Institute. Financing is based on an employee payroll contribution of 9% of earnings and an employer tax of 11% of payroll. There is an earnings ceiling for the purpose of calculating contributions.

Bag-Kur. Funding for this scheme comes from a tax of 20% of income according to the income class declared by the insured person, a 25% admission fee, and penalties, donations, and income from Bag-Kur-owned property.

Civil Service Fund. The major source of funding is derived from payroll taxes of 18% paid by employers and 10% paid by the employees. Other income comes from a variety of salary-based charges imposed on employers and employees. Any deficits are covered by general revenues.

Administration

Social Insurance Institute. SII is under the administration of
the Ministry of Health and Social Assistance.
Bag-Kur. Bag-Kur is also under the general supervision of
the Ministry of Health and Social Assistance.
Civil Service Fund. The social insurance program for civil
servants is administered by the Ministry of Finance.

Agriculture workers have been targeted for coverage by SII
since 1977, but most of these workers are not yet included in the
system. Some independent farmers, civil servants, the self-employed, and certain professional groups who are covered by
special funds are exempt from SII. The latter includes workers
in private banks and insurance companies and stock-exchange
establishments. Benefits provided under the special funds must
be equivalent to those payable under SII.

An important distinction between the three basic systems with
regard to financing is that deficits in the pension fund for civil
servants are covered by general revenues. Moreover, benefit
amounts are set by the Parliament. The SSI and Bag-Kur funds,
on the other hand, must be self-sufficient and their limited
resources result in low benefit levels. The variation in funding
mechanisms is one reason that the schemes remain administratively distinct.

Civil Servants. Government employees were provided old-age
pensions as long ago as the thirteenth century (Myers, 1961), but
the current system for civil servants was established in 1950 when
11 different schemes were consolidated under the Civil Servant
Pension Fund (Emekli Sandigi). In 1987 this fund covered about
1,450,000 workers. The number of beneficiaries receiving benefits includes 680,100 retirees and survivors and 4,690,000
dependents.

Self-Employed. In 1972 Turkey introduced the Organization
for the Self-Employed (Bag-Kur), which provides insurance for

self-employed small businessmen, craftsmen, independent workers, and workers in specified trades. Unemployed spouses of persons employed in agriculture and housewives may be voluntarily covered. Disability, death, and retirement benefits, as well as social assistance, funeral, lump-sum payments, and various other supplementary benefits are provided.

Bag-Kur was created to expand coverage to groups that were specifically excluded from SII. Initially the system brought coverage only to nonagriculture self-employed, continuing to exclude most of the large segment of farmers. (Some 56% of the economically active population were employed in agriculture in 1980 [SII, 1986].) In 1984 coverage under Bag-Kur was extended to include self-employed male or female farmers over age 22 who are "heads of families." Currently about 500,000 persons in the agricultural sector are members. The total number of actively insured persons rose from 940,000 in 1978 to about 1,940,000 in 1987 (Bag-Kur Insurance Institute, 1987). In 1988 there were over 271,000 old-age pensioners and more than 204,000 survivors receiving benefits (Attila, 1990).

Social Assistance. Persons who do not meet the qualifying conditions for benefits under one of the social insurance schemes may be entitled to an income-tested social assistance benefit. About half a million indigent elderly persons receive this state funded benefit, but the amount is very small (Heisel, 1989).

HEALTH CARE UNDER SOCIAL INSURANCE

Medical care for SII beneficiaries is provided through its own medical facilities. Pensioners pay 2% of their pensions to help fund the program. The Pension Fund for Civil Servants provides medical care by buying services from the Ministry of Health and Social Welfare. Until 1987 persons covered by Bag-Kur were entitled only to cash benefits in the event of sickness or illness. Since then the institute has begun expanding health benefits to all of its active and retired members and their dependents (Heisel, 1989) but this activity is restricted by a lack of resources.

SOCIAL SERVICES

Most services are provided by families and friends, but there has been some effort by the social insurance funds to help communities meet the needs of elderly who do not have access to traditional support. Most of the assistance has been in the form of homes for the needy elderly who are mobile and capable of caring for themselves. The SII began building rest homes in 1984 and by 1986 there were 20 facilities with about 3,000 residents (Heisel, 1989). Bag-Kur has also engaged in building rest and nursing homes for elderly pensioners, widows, and orphans (Madazli, 1983; Yazici, 1983).

FACTORS THAT RESTRICT PROGRAM AUGMENTATION

Although income and health programs for the elderly are well established in Turkey, only about half of the total population is protected. Efforts to expand benefits to more persons are proceeding but a variety of specific factors inhibit further growth. Most notable are the effects of such factors as the predominantly young population, reliance on family support and charity, family structures, women's networks, questionable need, administrative limitations, and reluctance to tamper with the status quo.

Expansive Population

Perhaps the most important factor that reduces pressure for programs for the elderly is the composition of Turkey's population. The type of population structure in Turkey is referred to by demographers as expansive because it has the combined characteristics of a large proportion of young people accompanied by a rapid rate of increase. The population has doubled twice since

1927, rising from 13.5 million to about 55 million at present. The expectations are that it will reach 92 million by 2025 (Heisel, 1989). The mean age is 19 and nearly 40% of the population is age 14 or younger, a rate that is almost twice that of other European nations (Heisel, 1991).

The relevance of this trait to programs for the elderly is that the high percentage of young people shifts government policy priorities away from the needs of older persons. Creating new jobs for young people is much more of a state problem than meeting the service needs of older people (Heisel, 1988; *Foreign Labor Trends: Turkey*, 1988). Government attention in health care is also more focused on reducing infant mortality rates than in developing geriatric medical care (Heisel, 1989).

A policy of restricting state expenditures for programs for the elderly is further supported by the knowledge that only a small proportion of the population is age 65 and over. While the absolute number of elderly has increased, the high fertility rates have kept the percentage of elderly persons at around 4% for many years (World Health Organization, 1988). In 1988 the proportion of persons aged 65 and over was 4.3%, which is projected to increase to 5.7% by 2005 (Kinsella, 1988). This is significantly below the often-used standard of 10% of the population over age 65 to be classified as an "aging population." The population over age 55, which may be a better indicator of old age in Turkey, was 9.7% in 1988 and is expected to reach 11.3% by 2005 (Kinsella, 1988).

Dependence on Family and Community

As noted, official government policy in Turkey affirms the family as the social unit with primary responsibility for the care of the elderly. This is consistent with social, cultural, and religious mores. Although reliance on the family to care for elderly members has subsided in recent years, for reasons discussed later, there is a pervasive understanding that government policy should be designed to bolster the role of family care. This tends to make the government very cautious in sponsoring programs that might be interpreted as undermining the family. Under these circumstances, the urgency of national, provincial, or municipal intervention is defused.

Duofocal Family Structure

A social characteristic that reduces the need for formal programs of care for older persons is a tradition of support among the elderly, especially women. The support extends beyond normal assistance patterns found in extended families to include friends and neighbors built on a lifetime of close relationships. The conditions for this support are set by a social system in which women and men tend to live very separate and distinct lives, forming lasting relationships with members of their own gender that carry over into old age. The system has been referred to as a "duofocal" family structure (Heisel, 1987).

Women and Widow Networks

An important additional aspect of the duofocal structure is that care for women and widows in Turkey is an extremely well-developed system of mutual support throughout their lifetime (Heisel, 1987). This is significant because the majority of the elderly are women (55% in 1980 [Prime Ministry State Institute of Statistics, 1987]) and, based on 1975 data, half of the women in this age bracket are widows (Heisel, 1987). A social awareness of this informal support system lessens the pressure for the state to assume greater obligations to organize support services.

Nuclear Families

Nuclear families comprise about 68% of urban and 55% of village family arrangements. This condition, which is characteristic of many developing nations, is often used to justify state intervention to fill in the gaps of diminished support for elderly family members. As discussed later, such an argument has also been made relative to rural elderly who have been left behind by children who migrate to urban areas.

In the urban areas of Turkey, however, this reasoning has a weak influence on policy because nuclear arrangements are usually the result of a mutual preference by parents and children. Recent studies have shown that the ideal norm for older persons is to live only with one's spouse (Emiroglu, 1985, cited in Heisel, 1989). Moreover, sons continue to be expected, and legally obligated, to provide economic assistance to their parents (Heisel, 1989). The nuclearization of families, then, does not necessarily adversely affect the ability or willingness of children to function as an extended family in terms of emotional and economic support, especially in cities (Heisel, 1987).

Questionable Need

Government policymakers apparently have accepted the conclusion that most elderly who are not protected for income loss and health care under one of the social insurance systems are either adequately cared for by their families or provide for themselves. An official at the Social Planning Department of the State Planning Organization recently wrote:

The elderly in Turkey do not constitute a group in major need of welfare support, largely because of the socio-economic and demographic conditions prevailing in Turkey. The social security programmes aimed at this target group provide a basic level of income for those minority of elderly that come under its protection.

In the rural areas, where retirement is not common, most of the elderly continue in gainful employment, and do not require support beyond that which can be provided by their families (Danisoglu, 1987:146–147).

Charitable Support

The need for state intervention is also diminished by a dependence on people to respond to the needs of the poor through
charitable contributions. This is consistent with the social and
religious tradition of alms giving. Under Islamic law the practice
of Zekat requires that one-fortieth of an individual's income be
given for relief of the poor (Prime Ministry State Institute of
Statistics, 1987). The extent to which this is practiced is undoc-
umented, but the expectation that local people will respond to
help needy elderly persons weakens any rationale for excessive
government involvement. A legacy of charitable institutions from
the Ottoman Empire are Mutual Benefit Societies. While, again,
there is little information on the number of persons covered by
these funds, their purpose and existence contribute to a perception
that state support is not warranted.

Social Assistance

As noted, social assistance benefits are incorporated into the
social insurance schemes to provide income-tested benefits to
destitute persons aged 65 and over who do not qualify for a
retirement pension and who have no one to support them (Sakdur,
1976). Although the benefit amount is small, the presence of this
type of program tends to sustain the notion that the needs of these
individuals are being sufficiently met given the limited national
resources.

Administrative Limitations

As noted, the Turkish approach to social insurance is closely
modeled after systems found in more industrialized nations,
especially those of Western Europe. A policy goal, then, is to
establish systems that have many of the features of the European
schemes regarding qualifying conditions, benefit levels, and

funding mechanisms. In some ways this goal creates administrative limitations that restrict the possibility of program expansion.

For example, it is generally recognized by government officials that the elderly population at greatest risk are agricultural workers because this is the group that falls outside the protection of the three social insurance systems. However, this concern has not been effectively converted into a workable programmatic remedy. The basic problem is in funding a system that meets the criteria of a fully funded pension program. The dilemma is the attempt to expand social insurance coverage to agricultural workers who cannot realistically be expected to assume the economic burden of making contributions.

While the SII is firmly committed to including agricultural workers under its program, the institution holds to the principle of maintaining the system as a compulsory, contributory system without government (general revenues) financing. Moreover, government officials believe that the imposition of a compulsory contributory system in the agricultural areas is both impractical and unjust (Danisoglu, 1987). An irony is that most of the European pension systems on which the Turkish policy goal is based are partially subsidized by general revenues.

The major objection in Turkey to including agriculture workers, however, is that a burden of payroll taxes would be unfair for workers with low income and sporadic employment, including variations caused by seasonal employment (SII, 1986). It is also argued that expansion of social insurance to many regions is not feasible because of a shortage of experienced personnel and because of the low level of education among potential beneficiaries.

Severance Pay

Any serious discussion of expansion or revision of social insurance raises the specter of unintended and undesirable changes for certain workers. One often perceived fear among workers is that revisions in pension policy will adversely affect the system of severance pay. Under Turkish law workers who are fired, laid off, or retired are entitled to a lump-sum payment of one month's salary for each year of employment (*Foreign Labor Trends: Turkey*, 1988). This can be a sizable amount of income and the trade unions have mounted resistance to proposed changes in the Severance Pay Fund Law in the past.

FACTORS CREATING DEMANDS FOR PROGRAM EXPANSION

Concurrent with the factors that impede program development are the pressures for the government to expand programs and revise provisions. Foremost among these incentives is the influence of government practices in the rest of Europe, the impact of returning migrant workers, increases in life expectancy, and the use of social insurance as an instrument of economic development.

European Influence

Historically, the impetus for the implementation of social insurance programs can be traced to the 1927 revolution and the subsequent reforms initiated by Mustafa Kemal Ataturk before the end of the 1930s. The reforms were designed to Europeanize law, language, education, and social customs; replace Islamic Law with the Swiss Civil Code; give women equal rights; and establish a secular state (Heisel, 1989). These reforms laid the foundation for the future establishment of social insurance systems that would also be modeled after European practices.

The adoption of a European approach to legal and social systems has tended to give credibility to European documents and proclamations regarding social programs and labor conventions. The Charter of the United Nations, which illuminates many of the European goals for social development, for example, had a direct effect on pension program development in Turkey (Myers, 1961). Another important factor in setting the parameters of pension policy are the standards for minimum social security protection under the conventions of the International Labour Organization to which Turkey subscribes.

The extent to which Turkey is influenced by European systems is evident in its interest in becoming a member of the European Economic Community (EEC) within the next five to ten years (Mercer International Conference, 1989). If accepted into the EEC, Turkey will have to adjust its programs for the elderly to comply with the standards imposed by the EEC. EEC membership would place considerable pressure for pension and health coverage to be expanded to currently excluded populations and would force some difficult decisions about continuing the practice of a pension system that is fully financed by contributions without government subsidies.

Urbanization and Nuclear Families

As noted, in the past the perceived necessity for government intervention in caring for the elderly was weakened by the presumption that their needs were to be met by extended families in what was a largely rural and agrarian society. This policy has become more ineffectual, however, with the rapid onset of urbanization and the expansion of the nuclear family. Similar to patterns in other nations, Turkey has experienced a mass movement of its population to the large urban areas. In the 35-year period from 1950 to 1985 the proportion of the population living in urban areas increased from less than 25% to 53% (Heisel, 1989). In many cases this has meant leaving the elderly members of the family behind. As a result, many rural elderly persons are bereft of the support from their children that they had expected (Heisel, 1989; Sakdur, 1976, 1977) and, consequently, become more reliant on public programs and services.

Today, extended families tend to be found mainly on middle-sized and large farms in rural areas. Both poor rural and low-income urban persons, along with upper-income urbanites, are more likely to live in nuclear structures (Heisel, 1989).

Migration to Europe

An additional ingredient to the pattern of rural to urban migration that plays a role in creating a favorable environment for public programs for the elderly is the large number of Turkish workers who migrated to Western Europe, mostly to the Federal Republic of Germany. This trend was especially prevalent in the 1960s and 1970s when about 60,000 workers a year migrated. The out-migration created a need for services by compounding the problems of reduced emotional and caretaking support when children moved from rural to urban areas. While economic support was often sent back home from Europe, the distances involved intensified the difficulties of maintaining a traditional family structure upon which many elderly persons had expected to rely in old age.

The importance of this aspect has diminished in the 1980s as the number of workers has subsided to less than 20,000 a year. However, a new concern has emerged owing to the large number of these workers who have returned home to Turkey. The number of returnees places an obvious stress on employment, but it also has a potentially powerful impact on policies affecting the elderly. The returning workers have become accustomed to comprehensive health care, social services, and old-age pensions, as well as a range of supportive income maintenance provisions such as family allowances and cash sickness benefits. These workers tend to be better educated and vocal and are less shy about making demands from the government to improve social welfare, including programs for the elderly from which they and their dependents will ultimately benefit.

Life Expectancy

Despite the relatively low proportion of elderly persons in the population, the number of persons aged 65 and over has increased dramatically in the past 30 years. From 1955 to 1985 the number rose two and a half times from 815,900 to 2,136,000 (Heisel,

1989). One reason for this rise is the increase in life expectancy at birth from 46.6 years in 1950–55 to 64.1 in 1985–90. Life expectancy at age 65 is estimated to be 13.7 years for women and 12.2 years for men (Danisoglu, 1988 cited in Heisel, 1989).

Social Insurance as an Economic Instrument

The accumulated funds of the Social Security Institute, which is a capitalization fund, consist of about 18% of the total savings in Turkey. This large resource makes it a forceful instrument in economic planning and development, especially in the provision of housing loans to covered workers. There are also discussions to use the accumulated funds for the creation of public jobs to reduce unemployment rates (Danisoglu, 1987).

In more recent years social insurance has been included in deliberations in setting five-year plans as both an instrument of social welfare and of economic development. A special department, the State Planning Organization, has been established within the government to promote ideas as to how this role might be enhanced.

DESIGNATED NEED AREAS

The government response to the various pressures to expand programs has been a moderate one based on principle of phased development in stages. The restraints noted above certainly contribute to a slow pace, but policy development is also affected by limited access to reliable information about the elderly population. In the 1970s the director of the Research, Planning and Coordination Department of the Social Insurance Institute asserted that available knowledge about the elderly was not based on sound data and investigations (Sakdur, 1976, 1977).

The issue areas assessed as requiring intervention, then, often rely on something less than empirically derived data. Within this framework, the issues that have been identified as needing government action include the problem of coordinating benefits among the three social insurance institutions, extending pension and health benefits to noncovered populations, and rising program costs.

Coordination

The issue that receives the most attention is the lack of uniform qualifying conditions and standardized benefits among the three separate pension programs (Sakdur, 1977; Danisoglu, 1987). The discussion centers on the virtues of adopting a uniform system that would distribute equivalent benefits on the basis of social equity or maintaining a system that empowers groups to effectively work to protect the best interests of their members. The question for the groups of workers covered under the Civil Servant Pension Fund and Bag-Kur is whether the level of their benefits would be maintained if administration of all programs were centralized under one government agency.

An additional impetus for resolution of the coordination issue is that a centralized administration might also address concerns over an imbalance in the dispensation of pension funds in favor of workers in urban areas (OECD, 1985). This is a reference to the use of funds from the three institutions to finance projects other than pension payments that is more generally widespread in urban than in rural areas. Presumably, a uniform fund would reduce some of the inequities in the distribution of funds because it would have to meet the needs of a more diverse membership who are more evenly distributed geographically.

Distribution of Health

The absence of coordination among the insurance systems also adversely affects the delivery of medical care. A Bag-Kur worker, for example, cannot obtain medical service from SII (OECD, 1985) because one cannot purchase medical care from a service that does not cover the worker's employment.

Extension

The problem of adhering to the constitutional requirements to extend social insurance protection, including health care, to the entire population is essentially a problem of covering agricultural workers and nondependent women.

Program Costs

A growing concern is a projected fiscal strain on the SII fund owing to the provision for early retirement. It is argued that the provision that allows workers to receive a benefit payment before the standard pensionable age is the main reason that the fund has a deficit. It has been suggested that these monies could be put to better use if they were distributed to more needy sectors (OECD, 1985).

STRATEGIES

Various strategies have been put into place to address the most commonly discussed areas of need. The primary strategy to provide economic protection is to build on the three basic social insurance systems, which also provide health care for pensioners and dependents. Responsibility for social welfare supports such as counseling, in-home care, housing, and food is predominately placed on the resources of the family.

Social Assistance

A current tactic to meet the goal of universal social security coverage without raising the tax burden on workers or making coverage mandatory in rural areas is to use monies from the SII fund to finance social assistance benefits for needy agricultural workers. The funds will be obtained by generating additional revenues for the SII fund based on reduced benefit expenditures that result from a higher retirement age.

In 1990 the retirement age under SII will rise to 60 for men and 55 for women. This is a reversal of two previous amendments, which first lowered the age in 1964 from 65 to 60 and 60 to 55, followed by a 1969 law that lowered it to 55 and 50. The 1969 law was designed to bring retirement more in line with the life expectancy rate, which at that time was 56 years (Horlick & Simanis, 1970). Presumably, the new law reflects the higher rates noted above.

Social Services

The government is also engaged in the gradual expansion of its involvement in establishing homes for the well elderly known as tranquility or rest homes and in providing assistance to the urban poor elderly. There are about 20 rest homes with a total of 3,000 residents (Heisel, 1989). In addition, the Ministry of Health and Social Assistance administers programs for domiciliary services and residential care for the frail elderly without family support (Danisoglu, 1987).

Coordination

The concern over an absence of standardized benefits among the three social insurance programs has led to several efforts to coordinate them (Sakdur, 1977; Danisoglu, 1987; OECD, 1985). A primary reason for this is to reduce the tendency for one program to campaign for better benefits than the other two. Each sector has worked to achieve the most favorable conditions for its members, including shorter duration of contribution and lower contribution rates. In 1969 such activity led to the lowering of the retirement age, which adversely affected the funds' fiscal stability (Sakdur, 1976). Another approach to increased coordination is to standardize the funding and benefits among the three basic systems to help reduce efforts to make one system better than the others.

Occupational Pensions

Occupational pensions play a very small role in the government strategy to establish income security for the elderly. A major reason for this is that employers are reluctant to make long-term commitments to a very young work force with inflation running around 75% per annum ("Social Benefits in Greece, Pakistan, Turkey Influence Adoption of Occupational Plans," 1989).

ANALYSIS

The policy objectives and strategies in Turkey for old-age pensions, including medical care for pensioners and their dependents, are primarily shaped by the government's determination to foster systems that are exemplary of the classic definition of social insurance. Within the parameters of this definition, old-age pension programs under the three government social insurance systems in Turkey are fully funded by contributions from employers and employees, coverage is compulsory for designated categories of workers, entitlement is based on contributions, and contribution rates and the level of pension benefits are related to earnings of the insured person.

Government policy decisions on pension protection reflect an effort to balance a constitutional requirement for universal program coverage with the desire to maintain a conceptually and fiscally sound social insurance program. The government's method of meeting this goal has been to adopt a stage-by-stage approach to program expansion. This is socially and politically acceptable in Turkey where pressure for more expeditious action is mitigated by a situation where the proportion of elderly population is low, pressing problems among young people are more pronounced, family and community support systems are strong, a perception of existing adequate charitable support programs is widespread, a relatively high level of insurance coverage of the more politically active and influential groups is in place, and expenditures that would add to the external debt are prohibitive.

There are, nevertheless, certain external variables that pressure the government to escalate its level of intervention. As in other economically developing nations, this includes an increase in the number of old (and very old) persons, rural to urban migration (including migration to Europe), and a growth in nuclear families. These factors have been influential in bringing governmental reaction to the increasing needs of the elderly in the form of marginal social service program innovations and pension revisions, but they have not yet overridden the constraints noted above that have kept government intervention on a rather even keel.

Government decisionmaking in Turkey relative to the goals and strategies of pension programs has, however, been uniquely affected by the country's aspiration to be closely linked to the European community. This long-range goal is clearly an incentive to develop a pension system that conforms to the minimum standards set by the EEC that essentially reflect those of the ILO.

A major concern for policymakers in meeting this goal is to address the problems of limited coverage and the inequities intrinsic to a system that is comprised of three separate and distinct programs. There has been much more successful activity in devising measures that gradually extend coverage and improve benefits under each of the systems than in bringing about formal coordination or centralized management.

The Turkish experience is of particular interest to foreign observers because of the methods being employed to extend insurance coverage to agricultural workers. Coverage of this population group is a major challenge for many Third World nations. The programs and provisions in Turkey provide an opportunity to observe the effectiveness of these measures.

Turkey also provides fertile ground for an examination of a phased approach to problem solving. An understanding of the process of needs assessment, goal setting, strategic planning, and implementation that functions under incrementalism in a developing country offers valuable lessons about program planning.

Finally, the Turkish system merits study because of the continuing attempts to centralize the management of the three insurance programs. Information on the pros and cons of such action, as well as the factors that promote and impede its occurring, are of considerable interest to social planners in other nations contemplating similar strategies.

8

Findings and Observations

In each of the five nations whose policies we have assessed, the governments have enunciated official concern for the well-being of older persons, but their intervention is circumscribed by a lack of resources. In each nation, the needs of children and youth are perceived as having priority, and policymakers genuinely fear that traditional family support systems would deteriorate if they adopted most social service programs, and some income maintenance programs, that serve the elderly in more economically developed nations.

A number of practical obstacles make it even more difficult to promote policies for greater government involvement in benefits and services to the elderly. These nations lack personnel trained in social service; their populations are often illiterate, geographically isolated, and largely rural; some have work sectors that are informal and nonwage-based; some suffer from ethnic divisiveness and government instability, and there are cultural biases against offering services and benefits to women that are similar to those offered to men.

At the same time, governments face demographic and social forces that compel them to define emerging problems and develop strategies to deal with those problems. These forces are producing increasing numbers of elderly, higher poverty rates among the elderly, migration of the young to urban areas, a shift to a wage-based economy, earlier retirement of the labor force, increased participation of the traditional care givers—women—in the labor force, and diminished family support systems.

In spite of these pressures toward government intervention, there are powerful social mores regarding filial piety and family responsibility for elders, and these mores create distrust and suspicion about some imported systems of benefits and services. This is especially true where there is little history of such services at any level of official jurisdiction.

These nations have only one important misgiving about health care services targeted for the elderly, if only because they have given little formal consideration to geriatric medical practice. That exception is nursing home care. Nursing home facilities are widely perceived as being an undesirable substitute for proper care in the family. The belief seems common that the medical model of care exemplified by most nursing homes violates the right of individuals to die with dignity. In published articles and at international meetings, analysts frequently state that individuals should be allowed to die in a state of activity in their home, rather than meeting death in a public or private institution.

Although the study countries have a similar goal—maintaining the ability of families to provide for their elderly members—they differ in the role that their governments play in meeting that goal. Among the five nations we have examined, China and Nigeria have the least centralized control over, or constitutional commitment to, national programs for the elderly.

In China, in fact, there is a concerted effort to decentralize responsibility in order to maintain community obligations for care. Nevertheless, communities are clearly under federal requirements to provide the Five Guarantees: food, shelter, clothing, medical care, and burial expenses. In addition, the Chinese federal government tries to sustain a culture that not only permits but expects its elderly to contribute service to their community and family.

It is more difficult to determine the role the Nigerian government plays in addressing the needs of the elderly. Most nongovernment materials suggest that the government has little fiscal commitment to programs for the aged and does not delegate authority to community programs. Further, Nigerians seem especially concerned about negative effects of industrial models of services to the elderly. On the other hand, official documents indicate that the government is interested in fostering income maintenance programs, and Nigeria is an active participant in international training and research meetings on programs for the elderly. In addition, Nigeria has recently proposed increasing the participation of its elderly in community programs, a tactic that is typical of Third World strategies that relieve pressure for federal intervention by strengthening the ability of communities to meet their own needs.

In contrast to China and Nigeria, the governments of Mexico, Turkey, and the state of Kerala, India, are legally or constitutionally obligated to address the needs of their elderly populations. This obligation is intended to express the government's commitment to social solidarity and meeting the basic needs of all the population, rather than to reduce family responsibility. In each of these societies the government has taken numerous actions to support, expand, or create social services, health care services, and income maintenance programs for the elderly. Each society is, of course, at a different stage of program development. Mexico has put most of its effort into expanding health care services to the indigent, including many elderly persons. Turkey has perhaps the most developed system of benefits for its elderly population, especially for income maintenance. Kerala has made impressive strides in health care for the elderly—including them in its program for universal coverage—and in meeting the needs of the low-income population through it unique income-tested program for agricultural workers.

In all five societies, income maintenance programs create much less resistance and apprehension than do health and social service programs modeled on those from industrial nations. Social insurance and social assistance cash benefit programs, especially old-age pension schemes, have a strong appeal. Coverage is now generally limited to civil servants, military personnel, and urban workers in large industries. However, Turkey and Kerala have successfully extended income coverage to workers in the agricultural sector. Moreover, Third World governments continue to ask international consultants for help in expanding and improving social insurance income programs. Clearly, governments are willing to experiment with models from industrialized nations, either adopting them in whole or adapting them to local situations.

Analysts have little data with which to evaluate how successfully the various programs and provision in these five nations have met specified goals and objectives. An exception is the pension program for agricultural workers in Kerala, which has been sufficiently examined to be called successful. Doubtless, other programs have succeeded in whole or in part in meeting their original goals, but evaluations have not been performed or have not been made public. If research about the value of transferring programs from one nation to another is to be at all viable, indigenous policymakers and international consultants must share the findings of their program evaluations.

In summation, this study introduces a research model for analyzing data about the development and objectives of specific policies, programs, or provisions affecting the elderly. The model includes factors that promote or impede government intervention and thereby provides a clearer indication of how viable a program or provision might be when transferred from one nation to another. The model is a policy process model, which identifies and explains the factors most useful to national policymakers and international consultants in making judgments about programs. The model borrows techniques from policy analysis in political science, sociology, economics, and social work. As a diagnostic instrument, it examines program issues, objectives, and strategies within the government jurisdiction and determines the obligation of the study country to provide social services to the elderly.

The study suggests that, to determine what modifications a program or provision may need when it is transferred from one nation to another, policymakers have to examine the conditions in the nation where the program was originally adopted, the options that were available, the choices that were made, and the success the program has had in meeting its goals and objectives.

References

Adeokun, L. A. (1984). *The elderly all over the world: Nigeria.* Paris: International Center of Social Gerontology.

_____. (1985). Aging and the status of the elderly in Nigeria. *Zeitschrift fur Gerontolgie, 19*(2), 82–86.

Adiseshiah, M. S. (1981). India. *Ageing International, 7*(6).

African Conference on Gerontology. (1984, December). *Recommendations adopted by the African conference on gerontology.* Paris: International Centre of Social Gerontology.

Ageing International, 16(2), 1989.

Aguilar, M. A. (1989). *Mexico.* Unpublished paper.

Alter, J. D. (1988). *Aging in India.* Unpublished manuscript.

American Association for International Aging. (1985). *Aging populations in developing nations: A strategy for development support.* Washington, DC: Author.

Anstee, M. J. (1989, June). *Statement of Miss Margaret Joan Anstee, Director-General United Nations Office at Vienna/Centre for Social Development and Humanitarian Affairs.* Statement presented at the XIV International Congress of Gerontology, Acapulco, Mexico.

Antal, A. B., Dierkes, M., & Weiler, H. N. (1987). Cross-national policy research: Traditions, achievements and challenges. In M. Dierkes, H. N. Weiler, & A. B. Antal (Eds.), *Comparative policy research: Learning from experience* (pp. 13–30). Brookfield, VT: Gower Publishing Company.

Attila, I. (1990). Progress in the activities of Bag-Kur. *Asian News Sheet, 20*(1), 7.

Babangida, I. (1987). *Address to the nation on consolidation budget 1987.* Lagos: Government Publication.

Bag-Kur Insurance Institute. (1987). *Statistical yearbook 1987.* Ankara: Author.

Baihua, J. (1987). An urban old people's home. *China Reconstructs*, *36*(11), 32–33.

Banister, J. (1987). *China's changing population*. Stanford, CA: Stanford University Press.

———. (1988). The aging of China's population. *Problems of Communism*, November-December, 62–77.

Barnes, D. R. (1987). Wives and widows in China. In H. Z. Lopata (Ed.), *Widows: The Middle East, Asia, and the Pacific* (Volume 1) (pp. 194–216). Durham, NC: Duke University Press.

Bell, S. (1985). Retirement and other group benefits in Nigeria. *Benefits & Compensation International*, *8*, 9–12.

Benefits in Latin America focus on politics, economics, social issues. (1987). *IBIS Review*, *1*(11), 12—13.

Care of the elderly and rehabilitation: Mexico. (1982). *International Digest of Health Legislation*, *33*(1), 29–30.

———. (1987). *International Digest of Health Legislation*, *38*(2), 265.

Castro-Gutierrez, A. (1988). *Financial aspects of pension schemes in Latin America*. Fourth American Regional Conference of the International Social Security Association (Buenos Aires). Geneva: International Social Security Association.

Chambers, D. E. (1986). *Social policy and social programs: A method for the practical public policy analyst*. New York: Macmillin.

Chander, N. J. (1981). *The legislative process in Kerala*. Trivandrum: The Kerala Academy of Political Science.

———. (1986). Political culture. In N. J. Chander (Ed.), *Dynamics of state politics: Kerala* (pp. 13–30). New Delhi: Sterling Publications.

Chawla, S. (1988, February). *The participation of the elderly in development*. Paper presented at the Expert Group Meeting on Policies and Strategies for the Participation of the Elderly in Development, Valletta, Malta.

China faces problems in social security. (1987). *IBIS Review*, *1*(8), 25.

Chopra, P. (1982). The paradox of Kerala. *World Health Forum*, *3*(1), 74–77.

Chow, N. W. S. (1988). Scope for reform in the social security system of the People's Republic of China. *Asian News Sheet*, *18*(3), 22–28.

———. (1989, June). *The Chinese family and support of the elderly in Asia*. Paper presented at the XIV International Congress of Gerontology, Acapulco, Mexico.

Chuanyi, Z. (1989). Mutual assistance funds expand in China. *Ageing International*, *16*(1), 21–22.

———. (1990, March 19). Personal correspondence.

Clark, R. P. (1992). *Power and policy in the Third World*, 2nd. ed. New York: Wiley.

Collier, D. & Messick, R. E. (1975). Prerequisites versus diffusion: Testing alternative explanations of social security adoption. *American Political Science Review, 69,* 271–290.

Cruz, M. G. (1951). The concept of social security in American countries. *Bulletin of the International Social Security Association, 4*(6), 207–210.

Danisoglu, E. (1987). Turkey. In J. Dixon (Ed.), *Social welfare in the Middle East* (pp. 130–162). London: Croom Helm.

Davis-Friedmann, D. (1985). Chinese retirement: Policy and practice. *Current Perspectives on Aging and Life Cycle, 1,* 295–313.

Day care for elderly women. (1987, December 16). *Indian Express,* p. 3.

de Lehr, E. C. (1987). Long-term services in Mexico: Homes for the aged. *Danish Medical Bulletin.* Special supplement. Series S, Quality of Long Term Care, 40–49.

DeLisle, P. (1989). Changing employment practices in the People's Republic of China. *Benefits & Compensation International, 18*(11), 2–6.

Department of Economics and Statistics (1986). *Statistics for planning 1986.* Trivandrum: Government Press.

Diaz, R. A. (1979). *Social security and demographic evolution in the American region.* American Regional Conference, Ottawa. Geneva: International Social Security Association.

Dierkes, M., Weiler, H. N., & Antal, A. B. (Eds.). (1987). *Comparative policy research: Learning from experience.* Brookfield, VT: Gower Publishing Company.

Diessenbacher, H. (1989). The generation contract, pension schemes, birth control and economic growth: A European model for the Third World? *Journal of Cross-Cultural Gerontology, 4,* 357–375.

Dixon, J. (1985). China. In J. Dixon & H. S. Kim (Eds.), *Social Welfare in Asia* (pp. 21–62). London: Croom Helm.

——. (1987). Provident funds: An assessment of their social security, social and economic performances and prospects. *Proceedings of the International Forum on Aging, Beijing 1986.* Washington, DC: American Gerontological Association.

Ebomoyi, E. W. (1989). *Status of primary health care for the rural elderly in Nigeria.* Unpublished paper.

Economic and Social Council. (1989). *Second review and appraisal of the implementation of the international plan of action on aging.* Report of the Secretary-General (E/1989/13). New York: United Nations.

Ekpe, C. P. (1983). Social welfare and family support: The Nigerian experience. *Journal of Sociology and Social Welfare,* (3), 484–496.

Ekpenyong, S., Oyeneye, O., & Peil, M. (1986). Nigerian elderly: A rural-urban and interstate comparison. *African Gerontology/Gerontologie Africaine, 5*(12), 5–19.

154   *References*

Emiroglu, V. (1985). Nucleus of older persons in villages (in Turkish). *Antropoloji, 12,* 87–120.

Federal Ministry of Employment Labour and Productivity. (1985). *Quarterly Bulletin of Labour Statistics, 1984-1 and 2.* Lagos: Author.

Foreign Labor Trends: Turkey, 1988. (1988). Office of International Policy, Social Security Administration. Unpublished document.

George, V. (1988). *Wealth, poverty and starvation: A world perspective.* New York: St. Martin's Press.

Gerardo, H. G. (1985). Employee benefits. In P. F. Shaw (Ed.), *Mexico: Labor and practice* (pp. 109–121). New York: Bureau of National Affairs.

Gibson, M. J. (1985). *Older women around the world.* Washington, DC: International Federation on Ageing.

Gibson, M. J. & Coppard, L. C. (1989, June). *Family support of the elderly: Policy and program implications.* Paper presented at the XIV International Congress of Gerontology, Acapulco, Mexico.

Gilbert, N. & Specht, H. (1986). *Dimensions of social welfare policy* 2nd ed. Englewood Cliffs, NJ: Prentice-Hall.

Gill, D. G. (1976). *Unravelling social policy: Theory, analysis, and political action towards social equity,* rev. ed. Cambridge, MA: Shenkman.

Groskind, F. & Williamson, J. B. (1991). Social insurance policy in India. In M. B. Tracy & F. C. Pampel (Eds.), *International handbook of old age insurance.* Westport, CT: Greenwood Press.

Gujral, J. S. (1987). Widowhood in India. In H. Z. Lopata (Ed.). *Widows: The Middle East, Asia, and the Pacific* (pp. 43–55). Durham, NC: Duke University Press.

Gulati, L. & Rajan, S. I. (1988). *Population aspects of aging in Kerala: Their economic and social consequences.* Trivandrum, India: Centre for Development Studies.

Habte-Gabr, E., Blum, N. S., & Smith, I. M. (1987). The elderly in Africa. *The Journal of Applied Gerontology, 6*(2), 163–182.

Hancock, M. D. (1983). Comparative public policy: An assessment. In A. W. Finifter (Ed.), *Political science: The state of the discipline* (pp. 283–308). Washington, DC: The American Political Science Association.

Hardiman, M. & Midgley, J. (1982). Social planning and access to the social services in developing countries. *Third World Planning Review, 4,* 74–86.

_____. (1989) *The social dimensions of development: Social policy and planning in the Third World,* rev. ed. Aldershot, England: Gower.

Heidenheimer, A. J. (1986). Comparative public policy studies examined: An odyssey in four parts. *International Social Science Journal, 108*(2), 159–177.

Heidenheimer, A. J., Heclo, H., & Adams, C. T. (1975). *Comparative Public Policy: The politics of social choice in Europe and America.* New York: St. Martin's Press.

Heisel, M. A. (1987). Women and widows in Turkey: Support systems. In H. Z. Lopata (Ed.), *Widows: The Middle East, Asia, and the Pacific* (Volume 1) (pp. 79–195). Durham, NC: Duke University Press.

———. (1988). Turkey: Europe's Asian link. *Consumer Markets Abroad,* 4, 4–10.

———. (1989, June). *Socio-economic development and policies related to the care of the aged in Turkey.* Paper presented at the XIV International Congress of Gerontology, Acapulco, Mexico.

———. (1991) Social insurance policy in Turkey. In M. B. Tracy & F. C. Pampel (Eds.), *International Handbook old-age insurance.* Westport, CT: Greenwood Press.

Horlick, M. & Simanis, J. (1970). Liberalization in Turkey. *Social Security Bulletin, 33(7),* 1–2.

Hoskins, I. (1988). Conference reports: Aging demography and well-being in Latin America. *Ageing International, 15*(1), 32–33.

Hottinga, J. (1983). Factors influencing benefit planning in Latin America. *Benefits International, 12*(8), 15–17.

Hui, Y. F. (1987). Nature and adequacy of formal and informal support programmes to deal with the problem of the aged. In *Population aging: Review of emerging issues* (pp. 84–90). Asian Population Studies Series, No. 80. Bangkok: Economic and Social Commission for Asia and the Pacific.

IBIS Mini-Profile. (1988). *Profile—Mexico.* Chicago: International Benefits Information Service.

Ijere, M. O. (1966). Indigenous African social security as a basis for future planning: The case of Nigeria. *Bulletin of the International Social Security Association, 19,* 463–487.

———. (1978). *The development of the African social security system.* Lagos: African Universities Press.

Inter-American Center for Social Security Studies. (1987). *Primary health care under Mexican social security: The experience of the IMSS-COPLAMAR programmes.* Geneva: International Labour Office.

International Labour Office. (1977). *Improvement and harmonization of social security systems in Africa.* Fifth African Regional Conference, Abidjan. Geneva: International Labour Office.

———. (1985). *Informal sector in Africa: Jobs and skills programs for Africa.* Addis Ababa: Author.

———. (1988). *Yearbook of labour statistics, 1987.* Geneva: Author.

International Social Security Association. (1981). *Social welfare policy and services for the ageing in Nigeria*. Unpublished government document.

International Social Security Association. (1989). Experience of Nigeria. In Committee on Provident Funds, *Tenth meeting of the committee*, Nairobi (pp. 95–100). Geneva: Author.

Jack, D. R. L., Adeokun, L., & Jaiyesimi, S. O. (1984). The image of the elderly in Nigeria. *Gerontologie Africaine/African Gerontology*, 2(9), 15–32.

Jones, C. (1985). *Patterns of social policy: An introduction to comparative analysis*. London: Tavistock.

Jones, C. O. (1984). *An introduction to the study of public policy*, 3rd ed. Monterey, CA: Brooks/Cole.

Kareem, C. K. (1976). *Kerala district gazetteers: Palghat*. Ernakulam, India: Superintendent of Government Presses.

Kendig, H. L. (1987). Roles of the aged, families and communities in the context of an aging society. In Economic and Social Commission for Asia and the Pacific, *Population aging: Review of emerging issues* (pp. 75–83). Asian Population Studies Series No. 80. Bangkok: United Nations.

Kinsella, K. G. (1988). *Aging in the Third World*. Center for International Research. CIR Paper No. 35. Washington, DC: U.S. Bureau of the Census.

Kirk-Greene, A. H. M. (1986). West Africa: Nigeria and Ghana. In P. Duignan and R. H. Jackson (Eds.), *Politics & government in African states 1960–1985* (pp. 30–77). Stanford, CA: Hoover Institution Press.

Kisilu, B. K. (1986). *Conversion of provident fund schemes into pension schemes*. Ninth meeting of the Committee on Provident Funds. XXII General Assembly, Montreal. Geneva: International Social Security Association.

Krishnamurthy, V. (1979). Social security schemes in Kerala. In International Labour Office, *Role of trade unions in social security in Asia and the Pacific* (pp. 273–300). Bangkok: ILO Regional Office.

Liang, J., Chuanyi, C., & Jihui, Y. (1985). *Chinese perspectives on aging in the People's Republic of China*. Tampa, FL: International Exchange Center on Gerontology.

Liu, L. (1991). The People's Republic of China. In M. B. Tracy & F. C. Pampel (Eds.), *International handbook of old-age insurance*. Westport, CT: Greenwood Press.

MacPherson, S. & Midgley, J. (1987). *Comparative social policy and the Third World*. New York: St. Martin's Press.

MacKenzie, G. A. (1988). Social security issues in developing countries: The Latin American experience. Staff Papers. *International Monetary Fund, 35*(3), 496–522.

Madazli, N. (1983, September). *Pension systems in Turkey.* Sixth regional conference for Asia and Oceania, 6-10, 35-39. Social Security Documentation, Asian Series, Number 71. Tokyo.

Martin, L. G. (1988). The aging of Asia. *Journal of Gerontology: Social Sciences, 43*(4), S99-113.

_____. (1989, August). *Workshop on crossnational research strategies in the developing world.* Presentation at the XIV World Congress of Gerontology, Acapulco, Mexico.

Mallet, A. (1985). The social security protection of marginal groups in rural areas: An international perspective. In *Proceedings of the round table on the extension of social protection to marginal groups in rural zones* (pp. 33–86). Mexico City: Instituto Mexicano del Seguro Social.

Mammen, K. J. (1987, December 29). Demographic slide-back must be checked. *The Hindu.*

Menon, A. S. (1967). *A survey of Kerala history.* Kottayam, India: National Book Stall.

Mercer International Conference: London. (1989). *Benefits & Compensation International, 19*(1), 23–28.

Mesa-Lago, C. (1978). *Social security in Latin America: Pressure groups, stratification, and inequality.* Pittsburgh: University of Pittsburgh Press.

_____. (1986). Comparative study of the development of social security in Latin America. *International Social Security Review, 39*(2), 127–152.

Midgley, J. (1984a). *Social security, inequality, and the Third World.* New York: Wiley.

_____. (1984b). Diffusion and the development of social policy: Evidence from the Third World. *Journal of Social Policy, 13,* 167–184.

Ministry of Labor and Personnel. (1986). *Readings in social insurance and employees' benefits* (in Chinese). Bejing: Author.

Mohsin, N. (1985). *Rural development through government programmes.* Delhi: Mittal Publications.

Mok, B. H. (1983). In the service of socialism: Social welfare in China. *Social Work, 28*(4), 269–272.

Morris, R. (1985). *Social policy of the American welfare state: An introduction to policy analysis,* 2nd ed. New York: Longman.

Mouton, P. (1975). *Social security in Africa: Trends, problems and prospects.* Geneva: International Labour Office.

Mouton, P. & Gruat, J. V. (1988, November). Extension of social security to non wage-earning population. In *Social security documentation: African series* (pp. 9–25). No. 9. Ninth African Regional Conference, Casablanca. Geneva: International Social Security Association.

Munoz, C. R. (1979). Mexico: Employee benefits practice and trends. *Benefits International, 8*(11), 8–17.

Myers, R. J. (1961, October). *Report on social security systems in Turkey.* Unpublished report prepared for the U.S. Social Security Administration.

Myles, J. (1984). Comparative public policies for the elderly: Frameworks and resources for analysis. In A. M. Guillemard (Ed.), *Old age and the welfare state* (pp. 19–44). Beverly Hills, CA: Sage.

Nag, M. (1988). The Kerala formula. *World Health Forum, 9*(2), 258–262.

Nair, S. B. (1990). *Social security and the weaker sections.* Delhi, India: Renaissance Publishing House.

Nair, S. B. & Tracy, M. B. (1989). Pensions for women in the Third World: A case study of Kerala, India. *International Journal of Contemporary Sociology, 26*(3–4), 175–188.

National perspectives on aging issues. (1982). *Bulletin on Aging, 6*(2), 8–21.

Nayar, P. K. B. (1983). Ecology, social welfare and mortality behavior: The case of Kerala, India. *International Review of Sociology/Revue Internationale de Sociologie, 19*(1–3), 115–136.

_____. (1985). Population aging in India: The background. In *International Seminar on Population Aging in India*, Seminar Proceedings, Trivandrum, February 3–7, 1–15.

Neysmith, S. M. & Edwardh, J. (1984). Economic dependency in the 1980s: Its impact on Third World elderly. *Ageing and Society, 4*(1), 21–44.

Nigeria. (1983). *Bulletin on Aging, 8*(1), 28.

Novelo, G. (1985). Actions of the inter-American conference on social security with regard to the promotion of social protection to rural populations. In *Proceedings of the round table on the extension of social protection to marginal groups in rural zones* (pp. 85–117). Mexico City: Instituto Mexicano del Seguro Social.

Nugent, J. & Gillaspy, T. (1983). Old age pensions and fertility in rural areas of less developed countries: Some evidence from Mexico. *Economic Development and Cultural Change, 31*(4).

Ogunshola, A. O. (1979). Social security and private pension practice in Nigeria. *Benefits International, 9*(2), 5–12.

Omari, C. K. (1987, November). *The future of the elderly in the African family.* Unpublished document. Iowa City: Center for International and Comparative Studies, The University of Iowa.

Onokerhoraye, A. G. (1984). *Social services in Nigeria: An introduction.* London: Kegan Paul.

Organization for Economic Cooperation and Development. (1985, May). *Social welfare policies in Turkey.* Office of International Policy, Social Security Administration document.

Oriol, W. E. (1982). *Aging in all nations: A special report on the United Nations world assembly on aging.* Washington, DC: National Council on the Aging.

Oyovbaire, S. E. (1984). *Federalism in Nigeria: A study in the development of the Nigerian state.* New York: St. Martin's Press.

Pampel, F. C. & Williamson, J. B. (1985). Age structure, politics, and cross-national patterns of public pension expenditures. *American Sociological Review, 50,* 782–799.

Panikar, P. G. K. & C. R. Soman. (1984). *Health status of Kerala: Paradox of economic backwardness and health development.* Trivandrum, India: Centre for Development Studies.

Pathmarajah, N. (1984). *Systems of old age protection in Asia and Oceania.* Regional Training Seminar on Social Security Administration, Kathmandu. Geneva: International Social Security Association.

Peil, M. (1991). Family support for the Nigerian elderly. *Journal of Comparative Family Studies.*

Peil, M., Bamisaiye, A., & Ekpenyong, S. (1989). Health and physical support for the elderly in Nigeria. *Journal of Cross-Cultural Gerontology, 4,* 89–196.

Peil, M., Ekpenyong, S., & Oyeneye, O. (1985). Retirement in Nigeria. *Cultures et Developpement, 17,* 665–682.

Petri, P. A. (1982). Income, employment, and retirement policies. In R. H. Binstock, W. S. Chow, & J. H. Schulz (Eds.), *International perspectives on aging: Population and policy challenges* (pp. 75–126). New York: United Nations Fund for Population Activities.

Pistirio, R. (1985). Summation. In Pan American Health Organization, *Toward the well-being of the elderly* (pp. 159–163). Washington, DC: Pan American Health Organization.

Poitras, G. E. (1973). Welfare bureaucracy and clientele politics in Mexico. *Administrative Science Quarterly,* 18(March), 18–26.

Prime Ministry State Institute of Statistics. (1987). *1987 Statistical yearbook of Turkey.* Ankara: Author.

Programmes for China's 80 Million Elderly. (1984). *Bulletin on Aging, 2*(3), 10–11.

Pye, L. W. (1984). *China: An introduction* 3rd ed. Boston: Little, Brown.

Rabasa-Gamboa, E. (1991). Social security in Mexico: The case of the Mexican Social Security Institute (IMSS). In M. B. Tracy & F. C.

Pampel (Eds.), *International handbook of old-age insurance*. Westport, CT: Greenwood Press.

Roberts, J. (March, 1976). State pension schemes and statutory retirement pay in Turkey. *Benefits International*, 10–12.

Rose, R. (1973). Comparing public policy: An overview. *European Journal of Political Research*, *1*, 67–94.

Rwezaura, B. A. (1989). Changing community obligations to the elderly in contemporary Africa. *Journal of Social Development in Africa*, *4*(1), 5–24.

Sadri, S. (1987). Taking on Unilever. *Review of African Political Economy*, *39*(9), 63–68.

Sakdur, H. (1976). Social security, social services and assistance for the elderly in Turkey. *International Social Security Review*, *29*(4), 355–359.

_____. (1977). Social services, social assistance and social security for aged persons. *Asian News Sheet*, *7*(2), 16–18.

Sanda, A. O. (1987). Nigeria. In J. Dixon (Ed.), *Social Welfare in Africa* (pp. 164–183). London: Croom Helm.

Sander, G. B. & Mendoza, F. J. C. (1987). Paying with chuchulucos: Creativity in compensation in Mexico. *Benefits & Compensation International*, *17*(6), 7–12.

Seager, J. & Olson, A. (1986). *Women in the world: An international atlas*. London: Pluto Press.

Sennott-Miller, L. (1989). *Midlife and older women in Latin America and Caribbean: A status report*. Washington, DC: American Association of Retired Persons & Pan American Health Organization.

Sher, A. E. (1984). *Aging in post-Mao China: The politics of veneration*. Boulder, CO: Westview Press.

Smeeding, T. M. & Torrey, B. B. (1987). *Comparative economic status of the elderly in eight countries: Policy lessons from the Luxembourg income study and the international database on aging*. LIS-CEP Working Paper No. 9. Luxembourg: Luxembourg Income Study.

Soberon, G., Frank, J., & Sepulveda, J. (1986). The health care reform in Mexico: Before and after the 1985 earthquakes. *American Journal of Public Health*, *76*(6), 673–680.

Social benefits in Greece, Pakistan, Turkey influence adoption of occupational plans. (1989). *IBIS Review*, *3*(12), 18–19.

Social Insurance Institution. (1986). *The national experience of Turkey in the field of social security protection for the rural population*. Asian Regional Round Table Meeting on Social Security Protection for the Rural Population. Geneva: International Social Security Association.

State Planning Board. (1984). *Draft, seventh five year plan 1985–90 and annual plan 1985–86, Vol 1. Trivandrum, India: Author.*

_____. (1987). *Economic Review 1986.* Trivandrum: Government Press.

Swantz, L. M. (1985). *Women in development: A creative role denied.* London: C. Hurst.

Sykes, J. T. & Sykes, K. (1986). Conferencia latinoamerica de gerontologia called very successful. *Ageing International, 13*(3), 16–17, 22.

Tamburi, G. (1985). Social security in Latin America: Trends and outlook. In C. Mesa-Lago (Ed.), *The crisis of social security and health care: Latin American experiences and lessons* (pp. 57–83). Pittsburgh: Center for Latin American Studies.

Tang, D. C. (1989, June). The aging problem in China. Paper presented at the XIV International Congress of Gerontology, Acapulco, Mexico.

Tapia-Videla, J. I. & Parrish, C. J. (1982). Ageing, development and social service delivery systems in Latin America: Problems and perspectives. *Ageing and Society, 2*(March), 31–55.

Tartter, J. R. (1982). Government and politics. In H. D. Nelson (Ed.), *Nigeria: A country study* 4th ed. (pp. 187–234) Washington, DC: American University.

Tax-effective benefits take spotlight in Brazil, Mexico, Central America. (1989). *IBIS Review, 3*(12), 20–21.

Teune, H. (1978). A logic of comparative policy analysis. In D. F. Ashford (Ed.), *Comparing public policies: New concepts and methods* (pp. 43–55). Beverly Hills, CA: Sage.

Torrey, B. B., Kinsella, K., & Taeuber, C. M. (1987). *An aging world.* International Population Reports Series P-95, No. 78. Bureau of the Census. Washington, DC: Government Printing Office.

Tout, K. (1989). *Ageing in developing countries.* New York: Oxford University Press.

TPF&C international seminar: Brighton. 1989. *Benefits & Compensation International, 19*(1), 29–34.

Tracy, M. B. & Pampel, F. C. (Eds.). (1991). *International handbook of old-age insurance.* Westport, CT: Greenwood Press.

Treas, J. & Logue, B. (1986). Economic development and the older population. *Population and Development Review, 12*(4), 645–673.

Tu, E. J. C., Liang, J., & Li, S. (1989). Mortality decline and Chinese family structure: Implications for old age support. *Journal of Gerontology: Social Sciences, 44*(4), S 157–168.

United Nations. (1983). *Vienna international plan of action on aging.* New York: Author.

_____. (1986a). *Developmental social welfare: A global survey of issues and priorities since 1968.* Department of International Economic and Social Affairs. New York: Author.

_____. (1986b). *African statistical yearbook, 1986.* Part 2. Addis Ababa: Author.

United Nations Centre for Social Development and Humanitarian Affairs. (1981, February). *Technical meeting on aging for the African region.* Lagos: Nigeria.

UNOV/CSDHA. (n.d.). *The United Nations programme on aging.* Vienna: United Nations Office at Vienna/Centre for Social Development and Humanitarian Affairs.

U.S. Department of Health and Human Services. (USDHHS) (1990). *Social security programs throughout the world, 1989.* Social Security Administration. Office of International Policy. Research Report No. 62. Washington, DC: Government Printing Office.

Vemea, E. S. (1982). *Gerontology in Mexico.* Unpublished paper.

Williamson, J. B. & Pampel, F. C. (1986). Politics, class, and growth in social security effort: A cross-national analysis. *International Journal of Comparative Sociology, 25*(11), 1–2, 15–30.

_____. (1988). *Old-age social security developments in Nigeria.* Working Paper Number 28. Unpublished document.

Wilensky, H. L., Luebbert, G. M., Hahn, S. R., & Jamieson, A. M. (1985). *Comparative social policy: Theories, methods, findings.* Berkeley, CA: Institute of International Studies.

Wolfe, M. (1968). Social security development: The Latin American experience. In E. M. Kassalow (Ed.), *The role of social security in economic development.* Washington, DC: DHEW.

Woodman, G. R. (1986, June). *The decline of folk-law social security in common-law Africa.* Paper presented at a Symposium on Formal and Informal Social Security, Tutsing, Federal Republic of Germany.

World Bank. (1984). *The development data book.* Washington, DC: Author.

_____. (1987). *World debt tables: External debt of developing countries.* Washington, DC: Author.

_____. (1989). *World development report 1989.* New York: Oxford University Press.

World Health Organization. (1988). *World health statistics annual, 1988.* Geneva: Author.

Xia, L. (1987). New ways of serving the needy. *China Reconstructs, 36*(11).

Yazici, A. (1983). Social security benefits: Improvements 1982. *Asian News Sheet, 13*(3), 1983.

Zimbabwe action plan on the elderly. (1986, December). *Proceedings of a Workshop on Planning for the Needs of the Elderly.* Harare: School of Social Work.

Additional Readings

Aging and the aged in the Third World. (1982). Williamsburg, VA: College of William and Mary.

American Association for International Aging. (1985). *Aging populations in developing nations: A strategy for development support.* Washington, DC: Author.

_____. (1988). *An international directory of organizations in aging.* Washington, DC: Author.

Andrews, G. R., Esterman, A. J., Braunack-Mayer, A. J., & Rungie, C. M. (1986). *Aging in the Western Pacific.* Manila: World Health Organization.

Asvall, J. E. (1985). The internationalization of gerontology: The role of the World Health Organization: past, present, and future. In Pan American Health Organization, *Toward the well-being of the elderly* (Scientific publication No. 492) (pp. 1–5). Washington, DC: Pan American Health Organization.

Avelar, J. R. de. (1982). *Social protection of the rural populations.* Second American Regional Conference. Caracas, November 16–19. Geneva: International Social Security Association.

Benda-Beckmann, von F., von Benda-Beckmann, K., Casino, E., Hirtz, F., Woodman, G. R., & Zacher, H. F. (Eds.). (1988). *Between kinship and the state: Social security and law in developing countries.* Providence, RI: Foris Publications.

Bhattarai, A. K. (1989). Social security programmes in India. *International Social Security Review, 42*(4), 479–488.

Binstock, R. H., Chow, W. S., & Schulz, J. H. (Eds.). (1982). *International perspectives on aging: Population and policy challenges.* New York: United Nations Fund for Population Activities.

Castles, D. E. (1981). How does politics matter? Structure and agency in the determination of public policy outcome. *European Journal of Political Research, 9,* 119–132.

Davis, D. (1988). Unequal chances, unequal outcomes: Pension reform and urban inequality. *China Quarterly, 114,* 223–242.

Dixon, J. (1982). Provident funds in the Third World: A Cross-national review. *Public Administration and Development, 2*(4), 325–344.

———. (1986). *Social security traditions and their global applications.* Belconnen, Australia.: International Fellowship for Social and Economic Development.

———. (Ed.). (1987). *Social Welfare in the Middle East.* London: Croom Helm.

Economic and Social Commission for Asia and the Pacific. (1987). *Population aging: Review of emerging issues.* Asian Population Studies Series, No. 80. Bangkok: United Nations.

Findlay, A. & Findlay, A. (1987). *Population and development in the Third World.* London: Routledge & Kegan Paul.

Fuchs, M. (1986, June). *Formal social security in Third World countries: History, legal framework and reform perspectives.* Paper presented at a symposium on Formal and Informal Social Security at Tutsing, Federal Republic of Germany.

Gibson, M. J. (1980, Autumn). Family support for the elderly in international perspective. *Ageing International, 3,* 12–17.

Griffin, M. J. (1986). *Employee benfits for national employees of multinational corporations in less developed countries.* Waltham, MA: Brandeis University.

Heikkinin, E., Waters, W. E., & Brezezinski, Z. J. (Eds.). (1983). *The elderly in eleven countries: A sociomedical survey.* Geneva: World Health Organization.

Heisel, M. (1985). Aging in the context of population policies in developing countries. *Population Bulletin of the United Nations,* No. 17. New York: United Nations.

International Labour Office. (1987). *L'investissement des fonds de la securite sociale dans les pays en developpement.* Geneva: Author.

———. (1988). *The cost of social security: Twelfth international inquiry, 1981–1983.* Geneva: Author.

International Social Security Association. (1982). Social security and the elderly: Background document prepared for the world assembly on aging. *International Social Security Review, 35*(4), 489–527.

———. (1984). *Committee on provident funds. Seventh meeting of the committee. Reports and summaries of discussions, 1983, Geneva, 10 October.* New Dehli: ISSA Regional Office for Asia and Oceania.

———. (1987). *Social security protection for the rural population.* Report of the Asian regional round table meeting, Jakarta. Social Security Documentation Asian Series, No. 11. New Delhi: ISSA Regional Office for Asia and the Pacific.

_____. (1989). *World bibliography of social security.* Geneva: Author.

_____. (1989). Developments and trends in social security 1987–1989. *International Social Security Review, 42*(3), 247–349.

Liangjin, C. (1990). Social development mechanisms and social security functions. *International Sociology, 5*(1), 89–100.

Lopata, H. Z. (1987). Widowhood: World perspectives on support systems. In H. Z. Lopata (Ed.), *Widows: The Middle East, Asia, and the Pacific* (pp. 1–23). Durham, NC: Duke University Press.

MacPherson, S. & Midgley, J. (1987). *Comparative social policy and the third world.* New York: St. Martin's Press.

Martin, L. G. (1990). The status of south Asia's growing elderly population. *Journal of Cross-Cultural Gerontology, 5*, 93–117.

Meegama, S. (1982). Aging in developing countries. *World Health Statistics Quarterly, 35*, 239–245.

Midgley, J. (1990). International social work: Learning from the Third World. *Social Work, 35*(4), 295–301.

Morgan, J. H. (1985). *Aging in developing societies: A reader in third world gerontology.* Bristol, IN: Wyndham Hall Press.

Myers, G. & Nathanson, C. (1982). Aging and the family. *World Health Statistics Quarterly, 35*, 225–238.

Myles, J. (1984). *Old age and the welfare state.* Boston: Little, Brown.

Naifu, C. (1988). Reflections on a social security system with Chinese characteristics. *International Social Security Review, 41*(2), 170–175.

Palmore, E. (Ed.). (1980). *International handbook on aging: Contemporary developments and research.* Westport, CT: Greenwood Press.

Perrin, G. (1985). The recognition of the right to social protection as a human right. *Labour & Society, 10*(5), 239–258.

Rondinelli, D. A., & Cheema, G. S. (1988). *Urban services in developing countries: Public and private roles in urban development.* Basingstoke, England: Macmillan.

Rubinstein, R. L. & Johnsen, P. T. (1982). Toward a comparative perspective on filial response to aging populations. In J. Sokolovsky (Ed.), *Aging and the aged in the Third World: Part I* (pp. 115–172). Williamsburg, VA: College of William and Mary.

Schade, B. (1982). Aging and old age in developing countries. In H. Thomae & G. L. Maddox (Eds.), *New perspectives on old age: A message to decision makers* (pp. 98–114). New York: Springer.

_____. (1983). Aging in developing countries. In M. Bergener, U. Lehr, E. Lang, & R. Schmitz-Scherzer (Eds.), *Aging in the eighties and beyond: Highlights of the twelfth international congress of gerontology* (pp. 383–390). New York: Springer.

Siegel, J. S. & Hoover, S. L. (1982). Demographic aspects of the health of the elderly to the year 2000 and beyond. *World Health Statistics Quarterly, 35,* 133–202.

———. (1984). *International trends and perspectives: Aging.* (International Research Document No. 12). Washington, DC: Government Printing Office.

Tracy, M. B. (1988). Integrating cash pension benefits and health services for agriculture workers in developing countries. In D. S. Sanders & J. Fischer (Eds.), *Visions for the future: Social work and Pacific-Asian perspectives* (pp. 149–163). Manoa: University of Hawaii Press.

United Nations. (1982). *Report of the world assembly on aging.* New York: Author.

———. (1982). *Aging populations and rural development.*

Report of the Food and Agriculture Organization. (A/CONF.113/8). New York: Author.

———. (1983). *Vienna international plan of action on aging.* New York: Author.

———. (1985). *The world aging situation: Strategies and policies.* New York: Department of International Economic and Social Affairs.

———. (1986). *Developmental social welfare: A global survey of issues and priorities since 1968.* Department of International Economic and Social Affairs. New York: Author.

United Nations Fund for Population Activities. (1982). International perspectives on aging. *Population and Policy Challenge, 7*(8). New York: UNFPA, Policy Development Studies.

U.S. House Select Committee on Aging. (1985). 2nd sess. 98th Cong. *U.S. Perspectives: International Action on Aging.* Washington, D.C.: Government Printing Office.

World Health Organization. (1981). *Global strategy for health for all by the year 2000.* Geneva: Author.

Index

ABOUT THE AUTHOR

MARTIN B. TRACY is an Associate Professor with the School of Social Work at the University of Iowa and a member of the University's Center for International Rural and Environmental Health. He is a former research analyst with the U.S. Social Security Administration and with the International Social Security Association in Geneva. He has contributed articles to the *International Journal of Contemporary Sociology* and to the book *Visions for the Future: Social Work and Pacific-Asian Perspectives*.